Florida Fishing

Allen Applegarth

Southern Heritage Press
St. Petersburg, Florida

Southern Heritage Press

Byron Kennedy, Publisher
P.O. Box 10937
St. Petersburg, Florida 33733
1-800-282-2823

Printed in the U.S.A.
ISBN 0-941072-14-3

Special thanks to the Department of Environmental Protection,
Office of Fisheries Management and Assistance Services and artist
Diane Rome Peebles for the artwork in the appendix and the
sport fish section of the book.

Book design by
Voshardt/Humphrey Artworks, Inc.
St. Petersburg, Florida

Prologue

Fishing in the Sunshine State can be an unforgettable experience. The sunshine is almost constant, as well as the fish. Over 4000 miles of coastline, not including inlets or estuaries, lure millions of visiting anglers and vacationers here each year. A vast majority of our visitors 'do not leave home without their credit cards, nor do they leave home without their fishing gear.'

Whether you are casting from a land-fixed structure or a boat offshore, at any moment you may encounter a lengthy explosive battle with the inquisitive moves and power of a 'snook, tarpon, or one of our other red-blooded torpedoes.'

For those fortunate enough to go deep sea fishing, you can expect an extravagant day of line-sizzling fun in the sun!

The purpose of this book is to give the beginning, visiting, or local angler a wide array of information on fishing in Florida. This book provides you with crucial details and helpful advice, thereby eliminating the need to keep numerous guides on hand. Each fish has its own personal biography too, condensed to provide only the most important data. Below are some of the helpful topics included in this guide:

- Top Water and Bottom Water Fishing
- Finding Deep Water Fish
- Fishing at Night
- Complete Guide to Game and Sport Fish
- Less Abundant and Unique Fish, plus Common Sharks of Florida
- Baitfish – Catching It and Preserving It, plus a Quick Guide to What Fish Like to Eat
- Lures – Which Ones Work Best
- Favorite Recipes for Cooking Your Catch
- Fishing Florida's Artificial Reefs – How to Get There
- Emergency First Aid Reference

Acknowledgements

All sections in this book were designed according to public response and interest. I have spent many months combing the coast – interviewing and visiting anglers, locals and beginners of all ages. To all of those who participated, I give special thanks.

The following people, all specialists in their fields, willingly provided reef charts, rules and the listed species: John W. Dodrill, of Environmental Protection and Division of Marine Resources; Keith Miritello, of the Florida Marine Patrol District 4B, Crystal River; Captain Maurice Radford, of the Florida Marine Patrol, District 4A, Tampa; Florida Department of Natural Resources; Gulf of Mexico Fishery Management Council; and the Florida Sea Grant College program, University of Florida.

Also thanks to Sammy Carter and the crew of the Mary-Ann, and Captain Larry Papolas of the MV. Odessa for providing valuable tips on deep water fishing; Dianne Peebles and the Department of Environmental Protection for the outstanding color pictures; James Kalis for his outstanding half-tone artwork; Lois Grandison, R.N., for her expert advice on first aid; James Mallette for his contributions to advertising; Byron Kennedy of Southern Heritage Press for his guidance on this book; and a final and most favorable thanks to my parents, Norma and Jerry Whitman, who were instrumentally inspiring.

S.W.B.R. Melissa…

Table of Contents

Precautionary Safety Items

For all boaters, the main issue should be safety first. Listed below are some helpful items to keep aboard or take with you on your trips at sea. One of these items may aid in your survival at sea.

- First aid kit
- VHF radio
- Signal flares
- Air and sea tracking device
- Matches
- Die markers
- PMLs (personal marker light)
- Flashlight and extra batteries
- Life jackets (for everyone aboard)
- Compass
- Gloves
- Tape (medical and repair)
- Towels
- Water and food
- Line
- Extra anchor
- Sewing kit
- Basic tool set
- Sunscreen
- Oars and dinghy
- Extra containers of gas and oil

When going out on the water, always tell someone on land the general area in which you'll be. Also tell them when you expect to return.

Know Before You Go

Fishing requires patience, persistence, know-how and the right gear. Most successful fishermen obtain all of these qualities and more.

You will need to know the whens, wheres and hows of fishing. One or two of these will not suffice and your fishing outing will turn in to a waste of your time. If you know how to fish and when to fish but not where to fish, you are not going to catch anything. Maybe you know how to and where to fish but when is the right time?

Some other factors include:

• Different color baits for different water color.
• Fishing during tidal movement.
• Fishing under the moon phases.
• Warnings and tips from the sky.
• Various bottom types.

And many more!

Also a very important part is knowing the fishing rules and regulations because ignorance is no excuse. Violators are not taken lightly. Be sure to pick up an updated copy of rules and regulations from your local bait shop.

It would be impossible to list everything know on fishing, so I've put together some of the most important information to guide you in the general direction of being a more successful and cautious angler/boater.

Water Color & Baits

There are many different opinions of this controversial question. Some say, 'the darker the water, the brighter the bait.' Others say just the opposite. Everyone has his own opinion, so most of us follow the majority and the experts, 'The darker the water, the darker the bait.' Look at it this way – when the water is darker than usual, the brighter bait fish tend to keep a lower profile, while the darker ones are more camouflaged and expect to swim more freely.

Most of us stay with the nature of things, while others come equipped with the flashy bait. Fish often find this unusual to nature and are more often spooked than lured. Stay with the way nature works and you'll stand a better chance.

Fishing During Tidal Movement

Many species use the tide as a personal servant, to bring food to them or take them to their destination point. Predators will find a good spot to hide for the incoming tide and ambush any food that passes by. They maintain their position for the most of the tidal movement, provided it keeps serving up a meal. When the tide slows to a minimum or peak tide, they will swim around, regaining energy or occasionally feeding. The same principle applies when the tide begins to move out.

Keeping the above in mind, you will need to find where they are hiding and present the bait as naturally as possible. Position your boat on the down side of the tide, casting into the oncoming tide and letting your bait drift back to you. Incoming tides are normally the best time to fish, provided that conditions are right.

*For more details see Reading the Water on following page.

Reading the Water

Reading the water generally determines your success when fishing for many different species. The surface can act as a mirror image of what's going on below. A rough surface surrounded by a calmer surface usually indicates a rapid change in bottom structure or a sudden change in depth. When the tide rolls from deep water over a sand bar, this usually creates a rough white capped surface, thereby indicating a sudden change in depth. This same appearance can also be seen in deep water, caused by a rapidly changing bottom such as canyons, seamounts, drop-offs, or pockets in the continental shelf. This action may be more of a bubbling effect with occasional white caps.

*For more information on deep water, see "Finding Deep Water Fish" on page 33.

The ability to read the water surface comes with experience. When you see a difference in surface appearance, take a moment to investigate – this will give you first hand knowledge. Another common effect that you may encounter is an oily surface. This occurs when predator fish are feeding below, as the oily content of the bait rises to the surface. This sign also determines what kind of fish are feeding below. Only fish with sharp ripping teeth will generate the oily slick, which will also attract birds to the area.

*For more information on these signs see page 23, "Locating Inshore Fish."

When and Where to Fish

The best time to fish is during a rising barometer on an incoming tide. Work the inlets near open waters. During slack tides, work the areas farther inland. Fish generally move into the bays, flats, and mangroves to follow the bait run. The bait pack up in these areas until the tide washes them back to open water. Predator fish will move to the inlets just before the tide begins to move out – ambushing the outgoing bait. Look for the fish to be on the calm side of the structures, conserving the energy that they would expend if fighting to hold position in the tide. These narrow passes act as a funnel, channeling bait into one targeted area. The predator fish go where the bait are most vulnerable – the narrow passes and turbulent areas.

Free-line the Structures

Find a structure (piers, pilings, breakwall, etc.). Larger fish will use these to conserve energy by resting on the calm side while hiding from the bait. Structures are also found in open waters in the form of natural or artificial reefs, rocks, or holes. Cast into the tide, letting your bait drift back to you. Keep your line under control, but do not guide it. Let the tide move your bait naturally. Retrive your bait just before it passes you; this helps to prolong the bait's longevity. The force of the tide may be too strong for your bait when retrieving it against the tide and will shorten its liveliness.

Note: look for areas of backwash or abnormal current. Cast just outside of these areas and let your bait get sucked in. This will cause your bait to become disoriented – falling easy prey – providing the tide is strong enough. This method is best used with live bait fish, however it will work with artificial baits also.

Moon Phases

Different phases of the moon affect fish, along with many other creatures, possibly even human beings. A full moon often leaves many anglers wondering what's gone wrong.

You may have heard the old saying, "When the moon is full, so are the fish." Despite many theories, this is not so. Why do the scavenger fish seem to bite more than others during the full moon? Actually they just adapt a little differently during a full moon. The moon acts as a big spotlight sending most fish into hiding. Bait fish tend to hide in hopes not to be seen by their predators, due to the extra amount of light. The predatorial fish hide to ambush the bait fish as they move from hiding. The scavenger fish do not hide and become more aggressive, due to a shortage of wandering bait. This gives you a seemingly larger amount of scavenger fish. The tide is also affected, which disturbs the nature of their habitat. As the phases of the moon change and the light becomes less illuminating, the fish begin to return to their normal activities.

Sky Watch

Predicting the weather is a complicated task that requires high tech equipment (especially in Florida). Nature has given us a few ways to help predict the weather without the help of equipment. This is in no way a sure thing, but more of a helpful guide. Here is an old saying that holds true to it's word. "Red sky in the morning is a sailor's warning. Red sky at night is a sailor's delight."

Look at the stars in the sky. If you see a large amount of stars, rain chances are low to none. This is true because there are no rain clouds to block out the stars. There is another saying that goes, "If the wind is low, any incoming rain is slow." This means, if there is rain present somewhere in your area, it will take longer to reach you, versus high winds that will move the rain clouds at a higher rate of speed.

Always listen to the weather report periodically when you are outdoors and especially if you are going offshore.

Water Temperatures

Water temperature is probably the single most important factor in the fish world. Unlike any other creature, fish are effected by as little as 1/100th degree of temperature change in water. Fish are cold-blooded, which means heat accelerates their activity and cold slows them down. Each species has its own tolerance level and can not survive long beyond that level, however; some will stay on the edge of their tolerance level to follow prey. Some species move to deeper water to stay warm, while others move to shallow waters of the flats to bask in the sun. Fish do not like the water too hot or too cool so they are usually found in the comfort zone, which is mostly in a range of 10 degrees of their tolerance level.

To learn the tolerances of each fish, it is a good practice to record the water temperature when you catch a fish. Take note for at least five of the same species and average them together. This will give you the predictable range for future reference.

To get the accurate temperature, you will need to know the depth of where the fish was, bottom, middle or top and measure the temperature at the depth. The surface may be warmer or cooler than the bottom or middle. Some fish will only take to a bait in a certain temperature and will not move to another for any reason.

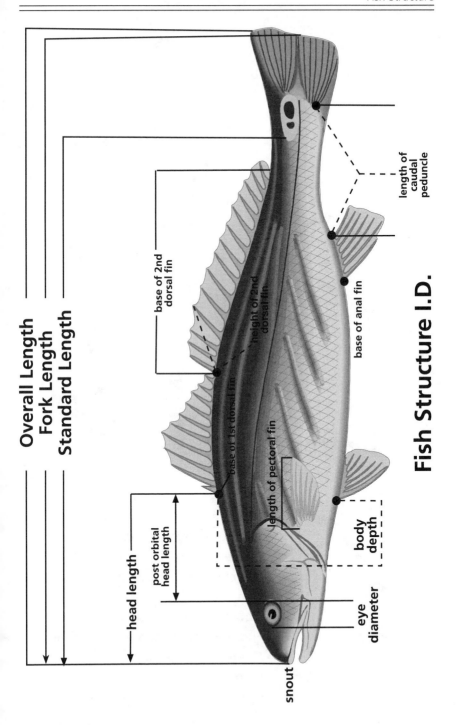

Fish Structure I.D.

Overall Length
Fork Length
Standard Length

head length

post orbital
head length

snout

eye
diameter

length of pectoral fin

base of 1st dorsal fin

base of 2nd
dorsal fin

height of 2nd
dorsal fin

length of
caudal
peduncle

base of anal fin

body
depth

Learning to Fish

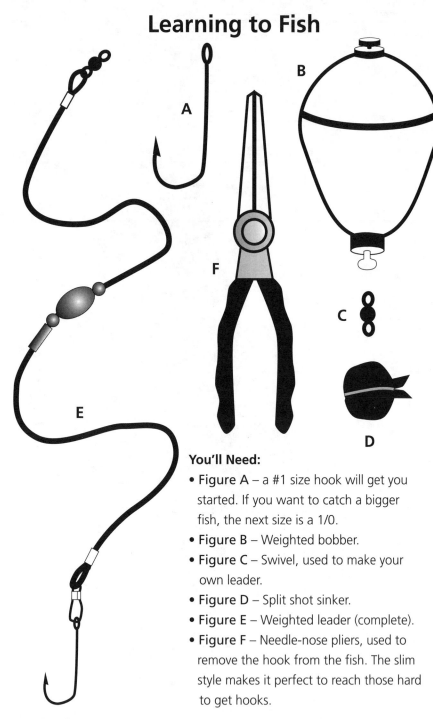

You'll Need:

- **Figure A** – a #1 size hook will get you started. If you want to catch a bigger fish, the next size is a 1/0.
- **Figure B** – Weighted bobber.
- **Figure C** – Swivel, used to make your own leader.
- **Figure D** – Split shot sinker.
- **Figure E** – Weighted leader (complete).
- **Figure F** – Needle-nose pliers, used to remove the hook from the fish. The slim style makes it perfect to reach those hard to get hooks.

Bottom Fishing

Practice

The first step is learning to cast your line into the water. To begin, tie a small sinker to your line in any way you want, but only a sinker and no hook. The best style is whatever feels most comfortable to you. You will want a close-faced reel because they are the easiest to use.

Leave about 6 inches of line hanging from the tip of your rod, push the thumb release button in, and hold. With your arm in a straight position pointing toward your target, bring only your wrist and forearm back while bending your elbow; your elbow should still be up and facing your target. Swing your arm back to the starting position, keeping your wrist stiff. Release the thumb button about halfway before the end of your swing; this will let the line out and will give it the proper arch to sail through the air, much like a ball when you throw it as far as you can.

After some practice, you will get the feel for it and will begin to use your wrist and shoulder for greater distance and better aim. Always follow through with your cast, leaving your rod extended out and pointing to your target until the bait hits the water. With some time and patience, you should be casting like a pro in no time!

Now you want to try your casting skill out on some fish…let's get your line rigged up for a day on the water.

Put a Hook on Your Line

We will need a hook. We will use a #1 size hook with a select size shrimp and a pea size clip-on sinker. First, we will tie on the hook using a fishermen's knot. Hold the hook in one hand with the eye of the hook pointing up. Thread your line through the eye and pull out about 2 inches of line and bring the threaded line together with the rest of the line, forming a loop. Overlap the end so that it crosses the main line and hangs over about 1 inch. Holding it where the two lines meet, turn the hook 4 full times in the same direction, keeping the line snug. Keep a hold on the hook and where the two lines

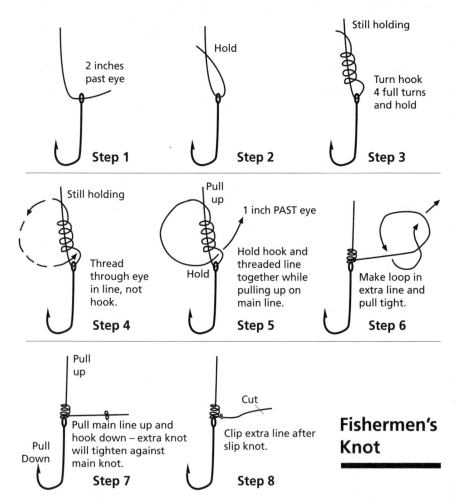

Step 1 — 2 inches past eye

Step 2 — Hold

Step 3 — Still holding / Turn hook 4 full turns and hold

Step 4 — Still holding / Thread through eye in line, not hook.

Step 5 — Pull up / Hold / 1 inch PAST eye / Hold hook and threaded line together while pulling up on main line.

Step 6 — Make loop in extra line and pull tight.

Step 7 — Pull up / Pull Down / Pull main line up and hook down – extra knot will tighten against main knot.

Step 8 — Cut / Clip extra line after slip knot.

Fishermen's Knot

meet; bring the end piece that is between your thumb down to the eye made of line, not the eye of the hook. Thread it through and grab it. With a hold on that and one on the main line, let go of the hook and pull both sides apart to form a knot. Pull snugly, not tight. Hold the hook in one hand and the main line in the other. Now pull the hook down and the line up, being careful not to hook yourself. By pulling both the hook and line, this will tighten the knot. With the extra line from the knot, tie a little loop knot using only the extra line. Pull the hook and main line apart until the knot is completely tight. The slip knot that you tie on the extra line should tighten against the fishermen's knot to prevent the knot from coming untied.

Add a Sinker

Now you're ready for the sinker. These sinkers are called split shots, or a more fitting name would be clip-ons. The sinker will be clipped on by putting the line in the slit of the sinker and squeezing together just enough to hold it so it won't slip off or up and down. If you squeeze it too tightly it will weaken the line. Place the sinker 20 inches from the bottom of the line.

Bait Your Hook

Now you are ready for the bait. Hook the shrimp in the tail. To learn this, look on page 96 for a diagram.

Cast and Reel in the Slack

You're all set! You are bottom fishing with this type of rig, so you need to cast away from any rocks or places that might have rocks. You may get tangled up on the bottom a few times, but you will learn how to read the water with experience.

Now that you have cast your bait in a safe place, make sure you reel in the slack in your line. Reel it in slowly until you feel a little pull; this will tell you that your line is tight. If your line goes out with the tide, you may need to add more weight to keep it where you want it.

Land Your First Catch

The moment is here – you get a bite. A bite will come in many different ways, but most likely you will feel a lot of little tugs and your mind will tell you to pull. Wait until you feel one long steady pull and 'let 'em have it.' Pull up and back, over your head, as hard as you can. This will set the hook.

You're almost there now! If you are having trouble reeling him in, try this. The fish will have the line tight. If not, you will need to reel him until it becomes difficult to reel any further. Pull up like you were setting the hook, but do it nice and slow and easy. With the rod tip in the air, let it down to the water quickly and at the same time reel in as fast as you can until it gets difficult again. Do the same thing over and over and guess what! You have landed your first fish...CONGRATULATIONS!

All About My First Catch

Date:

What I Caught:

Length:

Weight:

Location:

Bait:

Tackle:

Weather:

Remarks:

Top Water Fishing

Now that you have mastered the basic bottom fishing technique, you are ready to move on. Top water fishing is another fun way to fish. There are a few ways to do this. I'll show you two of the basic methods.

Free-Lining

This one is a pretty simple method. Tie a hook on using the knot that you learned before, and hook your bait the same way. Cast the bait in and you're ready to catch another fish. The bait must be alive and able to swim freely. It will be harder to cast because there are no weights, except for the bait. The bait will swim around, so you can let out some line to get it where you want it, or reel some in to keep it closer to you. Quite often the bait will swim to the bottom to hide. If your line stops moving, give it a little tug to make your bait start swimming again.

The line may begin to twitch a little; usually this is your bait running from the fish, so wait until you feel a steady pull. When your bait suddenly pops up to the top of the water and begins to swim in circles or jump, be still and you'll probably see the fish that scared your bait. Be patient and you will catch him.

Using a Bobber

The bobber will go in the same place where you placed the sinker in the bottom fishing method. There are no weights added to the line. If you need a weight, some of the bobbers are weighted on the bottom to get a better cast and stay upright. The bobber method will keep your bait from going to the bottom where they like to hide. The bobber should float on the surface unless you get a bite, then it will go under for a period of time. This is when you set the hook. If your bait can pull the bobber beneath the surface and hold it there, you will need a larger bobber. The bobber method is the most common way to top-water fish.

Summary

At this point you should know how to:
- Tie a fishermen's knot
- Bait your hook
- Add a bobber or sinker in its proper place
- Cast your line
- Use the bottom, free-line, and bobber methods

Keep in Mind

A lot of saltwater fish have sharp teeth and can cut your line with no problem. In these cases you need a leader. This is just a heavier piece of line or wire tied to the end of your line. Leaders come with and without weights. If you want a weighted leader, choose a few different size weights for calmer or swifter tides. The leader will come fully equipped with a weight, snap swivel, and swivel at the top to tie onto your line using a fishermen's knot. You will use the leader in the same way you bottom fish, but now you will have added protection against fish with sharp teeth.

The next way to outsmart a fish is to free-line with a weightless leader. This is just a wire with a swivel on one end and a snap swivel on the other to secure your hook. You will tie it the same as the others and use the top water method to fish. Leaders also come in mono line, which is used to catch the smarter fish that are spooked by wire leaders. Again, use the same proceedure as with a wire leader.

You have just graduated from the basics of fishing. This information will get you started and you will learn more as you continue to fish. One day it will be your turn to teach someone else. In the future, refer to this book for other tips that will continue to improve your luck.

Catching & Preserving Bait

There are two ways to get your bait. One is to buy it and the obvious is to catch your own. If you decide to buy your bait, there are a few things to think about. How long has the bait shop had the bait in their tanks? How long did the party that caught the bait actually have it before taking it to the bait shop? These are several factors that determine the health and longevity of the bait. Note: Most baitshops keep lively bait, just learn what to look for.

Let's say you wanted to have fish for dinner. Would you want a fresh, spunky fish, or a sluggish, weak fish? Fish are basically the same in that aspect, and would rather have the spunky bait.

Preserving your bait requires some knowledge and the right equipment. Most fishermen prefer the usefulness of a bait well, but a well is not portable. If you are using a portable bucket, however, an aerator is ideal for you. It is a battery-operated mechanism that produces oxygen in the water which, in turn, gives the bait longer life. Beyond lack of oxygen, the wrong water temperature will do just as much damage to your bait. The aerator is best used for transporting and nothing else. Bait must have a constant flow of new water to keep the temperature stable. I recommend an aerator to transport your bait until you've reached your destination. Then, submerse and leave your bucket in the water until you need it. Remember to put it back immediately after use.

- *Use an aerator to transport bait.*
- *Keep water temperature equal to sea water.*
- *Leave bucket in sea water until needed and return immediately after use.*
- *Don't overcrowd your bucket with too much bait.*
- *Remove all dead bait and keep bucket clear of direct sunlight.*

Cast Netting

Cast netting is a method that produces a larger amount of bait in less time. The best places to net are around boat ramps, piers, docks, grass flats and shorelines, as well as sea walls (if you can control your net). When using a small net (4-6 feet), you will have a better chance keeping to fairly shallow water, around 3 feet or less. Find a spot to net and toss in a handful of fine, strained chum or small pieces. Give the bait time to be lured to the chum and proceed to net, chumming between every other cast. If you are out during a low tide, look for a pocket of water where the bait is trapped. Usually the tide will drop below the bottom surface in many areas, trapping the bait in a small water hole and leaving you with a choice pick.

Spool of Line with Hook

Another method is to use a spool of line with a small hook (#10-#12). Tip the hook lightly with shrimp or your preference and drop the hook about midway to the bottom, leaving it in one spot.

When fishing in deep water, you can use the ocean as your personal bait bucket. Bait will hide around anything that provides safety from other fish. Take one of your own live bait fish and hook it forward of the dorsal fin. Attach a line and drop it next to your boat, giving enough line for it to swim only to the middle of your haul. This method will lure other bait in the area and your boat will function as the local hide-out. This will also lure the predators. Be sure to use an unappealing hook for your luring fish to keep the predators from eating your lure.

Once you have a fair amount of bait under your boat, use a light rod and reel with a small hook to catch your bait. The bait will usually follow the stray and stay beneath your boat. Toss in a little chum here and there to keep them feeding.

Chumming

Chumming is a method used profusely throughout the world by many anglers. It is most effective and increases your chance of catching fish. Anglers have different methods, but they are all basically the same.

To start, you will need a chum bag or mesh bag. Bags come with different sized holes and are chosen simply by your own preference. The holes determine how much chum will be released over a period of time. You will need a frozen block of chum, preferably menhaden, bluerunner, or mackerel guts. They are very oily and offer a much more alluring treat than others. Drop the chum in the bag and close off the opening. Attach a line to secure the bag to the boat. You may either hang the bag off the bow and fish within the chum line, or hang it next to you and fish the beginning of the line.

As the chum begins to thaw, it will slip past the holes and be released in the water. This will create what we call a chum line. After a period of time, you will notice an oily film, known as a chum slick, on top of the water. Add a new block of chum when the old one is down to about a quarter full; this will keep the chum line constant. As you are using the bag method, you can cut up some bait and hand chum for a bit of icing on the cake!

There is a pitfall to chumming, however. It will lure unwanted fish and limit your chances for the targeted fish. Not to worry, though, as we have a deterrent for this situation. Secure a weight to the bottom of the bag, leaving about 2 feet between weight and bag. Drop the bag to the bottom and pull up slack so the bag is off of the bottom and the weight remains. This will keep most of the fish to the bottom and allow you to drop in on the targeted fish.

A meat grinder is a great addition to your chumming equipment. This can be used to grind up unwanted bait for hand chum. Also, a bottle with an adjustable flow spout filled with fish oil is excellent for top water dripping. Adjust the flow to about 1 drip every 3 seconds and hang over the water.

Locating Inshore Fish

As we all know, every sea creature must consume some type of food, and to find the fish, we need to find their food.

There are many types of bait and fish, so we have to narrow down the prospects. Let's say you want to catch a cobia, and the time of year is spring. Since cobia move to the flats in the spring (see the game fish section), that's where you'll go. Look for head wakes, running bait fish, moving water, stingrays or dorsal fins protruding from the water. If none of these signs exist, then look for birds diving into the water. If they are diving occasionally, this usually indicates fish with little or no teeth, since the fish swallow them whole and leave no leftovers. If the birds are diving in a frenzy, this indicates the fish have sharp teeth and rip the bait up, leaving leftovers for the birds.

When looking for fish you will need to know the general information on the fish and the habitats of each species, while taking into account the weather conditions.

Listed below are 5 steps to locating fish. Follow these steps in order:

1) Recognize the time of year and water temperature.
2) Know the locating signs for intended fish.
3) Know the general habitat (consider step 1).
4) Know the comfort zones for intended fish. Keep in mind that steps 1 and 4 are vital for locating fish. Their habitat will change to adapt to different weather conditions.
5) Know their favorite bait and locate a school of it, or go to bait 'hangouts.'

The best way to learn how to locate fish is to follow these steps and record all pertinent information when you catch a fish. Take notes for at least 5 fish of the same species and average them together. This will give you a guide for future reference.

Deep Water Fishing – Fish and Tactics

Finding Deep Water Fish

Wrecks and reefs are home to large bottom fish such as grouper and snapper. They also act as feeding grounds for other nearby fish due to the large amount of bait fish surrounding the reef.

Floating debris such as: logs, pallets, weed lines, and even bottles. Take a few minutes to fish around, both the top and bottom of the water. Bait will use this floating debris as a means of safety and the big fish will be following close behind.

Color or temperature breaks in the water surface indicates the edge of a current flow, always a good place to find bait and their predators. Work both sides of the current edge.

Current is channeled or concentrated due to rapidly changing bottoms such as canyons, seamounts, drop offs or pockets in the continental shelf which create smooth areas bordered by rough areas with white-caps. Bait fish get caught in this rough current and become disoriented and trapped, falling prey to their predators.

Oil drilling platforms are home to many species of fish. The baitfish use platforms for safe cover, making them magnets for predators and fishermen.

Smooth oily slicks on the surface of the water is a sure sign that fish are feeding below. The slick is caused by the wounded fish, whose oily content rises to the surface.

A buoy and its mooring line are a lure for bait fish and predators. The longer the buoy has been in the water, the better home it makes due to marine growth on its surface.

Seamounts or ridges on the bottom will deflect the current toward the surface creating a temperature drop and upwelling nutrients that form plankton blooms, a natural attraction for bait and predators.

Deep Water Grouper Fishing

With these fish you must be patient. Some, such as the black grouper, will travel from reef to reef and others, such as the Warsaw grouper, will often stake claim to just one reef. Overall, they are extremely well camouflaged predators with a tremendous amount of power and acceleration, not to mention a 'healthy set of chompers!' Once they sink their needle sharp inward-folding teeth into their prey, escape is virtually impossible. They strike quickly and hit fiercely; attention at all times is a must.

When baiting your hook, don't be afraid to use an extra-large bait, for grouper are well equipped to handle such a hearty meal. A large, frisky bait will usually shift them into overdrive.

Using the right tackle is always of great importance, but especially when trying to catch one of these guys. Use a strong leader, reasonable for the intended size of the fish. A stainless steel 8/0 off set live bait hook proportioned to the size of the bait is standard for palm sized runners. The size of the hook will increase with the size of the bait and intended catch.

A common maneuver for a hooked grouper is to find a hole and wedge itself within to avoid being someone's dinner. Once you have been beaten by the grouper, chances are you will not get him up again. Follow the steps below and you may have a second chance, if you're lucky.

Let out some slack and put your rod in the holder for approximately five minutes, allowing the grouper time to cool down. Pick the rod up and retrieve the standing slack without putting any tension on the line, or else he may get spooked again. With your rod tip in the water and all standing slack out of your line, take a deep breath and pull like you've never pulled before. If you get him from the rocks, keep his head up and get him to a safe range, far from the bottom! 75% of the fight will be getting the grouper off the bottom, the rest will become easier as he gets closer to the surface.

When fishing these areas, be sure to fish at different depths and distances to find the 'hot spots.'

• Yellowfin Grouper
Color appendix A

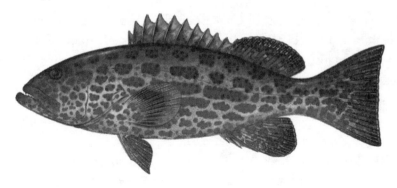

Yellowfin is a first class fish, and when landed, yields more weight than any other species of grouper.

The average weight is around 12-15 pounds, with many reaching the 45 pound class. Above 30 pounds, they are often called 'mustangs.'

At the top of their favorite menu, fresh squid wins the prize for bait most likely to be eaten first, with mullet in close contention. More com-monly used as bait are the grey and golden tile fish, which are the pinfish of deep waters.

When fishing in deep water of 300-500 feet, yellowfin will be in an area between the shell and sand which is found just before an abrupt change in depth. Before you hit the change in depth there is always the hardest bot-tom. Between this hard bottom and the adjacent shell is a sandy area. The bait always gather in schools over this sandy bottom, while the predators live over the hard bottom.

• Warsaw Grouper
Color appendix A

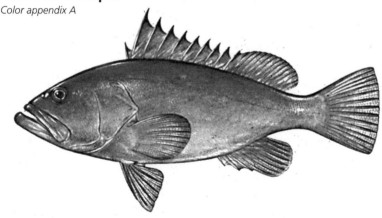

The Warsaw grouper is the largest of the offshore grouper family, with some in the 600 pound range, and many growing up to 1500 pounds. This is indeed the most notorious of the grouper family, and stories abound of giant Warsaw inhaling divers for a meal.

They are found mostly in depths of 300 feet to 2000 feet around ship-wrecks. Warsaw will eat almost anything they can swallow.

• Nassau Grouper
Color appendix A

The harvest of this fish is prohibited. Adults are found offshore around rocky reefs. Most catches are under 10 pounds. Sorry, but due to the protection of this fish, additional information is withheld.

• Yellowmouth Grouper
Color appendix A

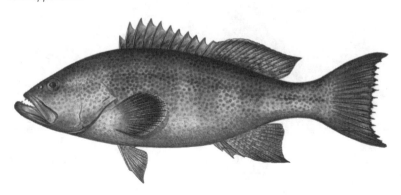

Most abundant in southern Florida, around offshore reefs and rocks. The yellowmouth feeds mainly on small fish and crustaceans. The average size is 15 pounds, but catches exceeding 30 pounds have been reported. It is similar to the Scamp but less dominant.

• Gag Grouper
Color appendix A

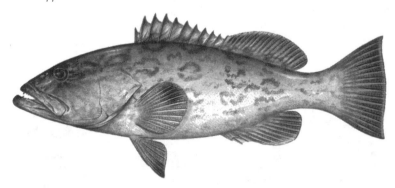

This fish is most often confused with the Black Grouper. The black and Gag grouper are widely sought fish being taken mainly with squid, but they will also take to a lively baitfish with no hesitation. Adults are found offshore around rocks and reefs. The Gag is more stationary than most of the species. They reach sizes over 70 pounds, but sizes ranging from 25 to 30 pounds are more common.

• **Red Grouper**
Color appendix A

The red grouper is one that is rarely found out of its comfort zone, between 66° and 77° F. They are bottom dwellers of the hard bottoms and feed mostly on squid and crustaceans. Average size is 12 to 15 pounds, but can exceed well into the 30 pound range.

• **Black Grouper**
Color appendix A

Black grouper is often confused with the Gag grouper. The black grouper is one of the more challenging of the species. Common sizes of 40 pounds and can exceed well over 100 pounds. Mostly found in waters over 100 feet, around rocky bottoms and drop-off ledges. Feeds mainly on fish and squid.

Deep Water Snappers

The snapper family offers a wide array of different snappers, but all look basically the same.

The most recognizable trait of the snappers are the two enlarged canines on both sides of the front, upper and lower sections of the mouth.

They are very smart and will take the bait on the opposite end of the hook, leaving you with only a tidbit.

They will often school up and can be caught in great numbers during a feeding frenzy. With these fish a strong leader and hook are required tackle for a successful catch. Most of the deep water species are all red in color, while inshore snapper will change somewhat to blotchy patterns or two-tone colors.

• Red Snapper
Color appendix B

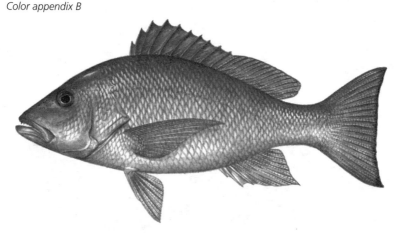

The swiftest in the family, red snapper just seem to know how not to get caught. When they are outwitted, they are primarily caught using Key West grunt. Most plentiful in Mexico. Average size of 5-10 pounds with a 3-5 pounder being a showcase snapper; can exceed 40 pounds. Can be found in 150 feet or deeper waters around rocks, reefs, and wrecks. This member is the most aggressive of the species. Red snapper are a highly valued fish, equally so for their taste.

• Blackfin Snapper
Color appendix B

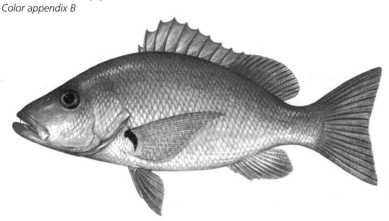

This fish is often marketed as Red Snapper and carries the general traits of other snappers. It is quick to take a properly rigged bait and will often turn away a sloppy rig. Found mainly near continental shelves. Grows to 20 inches or better and feeds primarily on small bait fish.

• Dog Snapper
Color appendix B

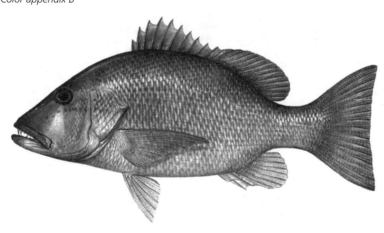

This large snapper attains an average weight of 10 to 15 pounds but can exceed 30 pounds. Known as a vicious nighttime feeder, it takes greatly to fish, crustaceans, and mollusks. Mainly found over coral and rocky reefs.

• Silk Snapper
Color appendix B

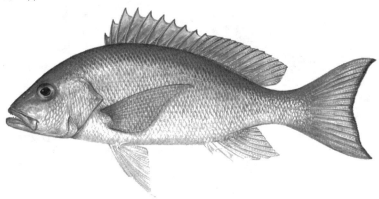

Little is known about this fish. It is found over rocky ledges in very deep water, mainly in south Florida. Average size is usually less than 5 pounds and it has been known to feed on any passing bait that cannot eat him.

• Cubera Snapper
Color appendix C

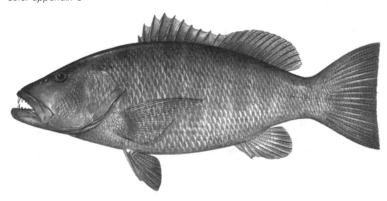

The largest of the snapper family and quite a treat to catch. Will grow well beyond 100 pounds, but more common are those in the 40 to 50 pound range. Adults are found offshore over wrecks, reefs, and ledges. Feeds on large fish and crustaceans.

Finding Deep Water Fish

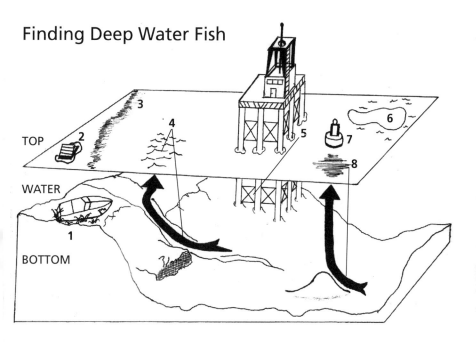

1) Wrecks and reefs are home to large bottom fish, such as grouper and snapper. These areas also act as feeding grounds for many other fish due to the large amount of bait and fish surrounding the reef.

2) Floating debris, such as logs, pallets, weed lines, and even bottles. Take a few minutes to fish around, on top and bottom of water. Bait will use this floating debris as a means of safety and fish will follow the bait.

3) Color or temperature breaks in water surface indicate the edge of a current flow, always a good place to find bait and their predators. Work both sides of the break.

4) Current is channeled or concentrated due to a rapidly changing bottom such as canyons, seamounts, drop-offs or pockets in the continental shelf which create a smooth but rough effect or whitecaps. Baitfish get caught in this rough current and become disoriented and trapped, thus falling easy prey to their predators.

5) Oil drilling platforms art home to a lot of different species. The baitfish use this for safety and basically the platform becomes a magnet for predators and fishermen.

6) Smooth oily slicks on the surface of the water is a sure sign that fish are feeding below. The slick is caused by the wounded fish; the oily content of the bait forms a slick.

7) A buoy and its mooring line are both luring to baitfish and predators. The longer the buoy has been in the water, the better home it makes due to marine growth.

8) Seamounts or ridges on the bottom will deflect the current toward the surface, thereby creating a temperature drop and bringing nutrients upward.

TIP: When fishing these areas, be sure to fish at different depths and distances to find the hot spots.

High Wind Drift Fishing

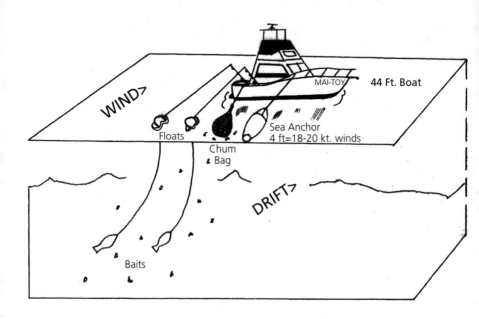

High wind drift fishing can become a real hassle, but when the wind kicks up, many of us ride it out and do the best we can. This guide will help you gain control of those nasty high winds.

The sea anchor must be secured to the center of the boat to keep it in balance with the wind and current. In winds of 18-20 knots, a 4 foot (wide end diameter) is well balanced for a 38-45 foot boat. To make sure your drift speed is not too fast, watch your chum slick, as it should stay with the boat. A sea anchor must be used properly to ensure stability, correct speed, line spacing of your rigs, these are all important factors in the art of drift fishing. It is always best to have a variety of sea anchors to adjust with varying wind speeds or to use an extra one as a counter-action.

Trolling Spread for Kings

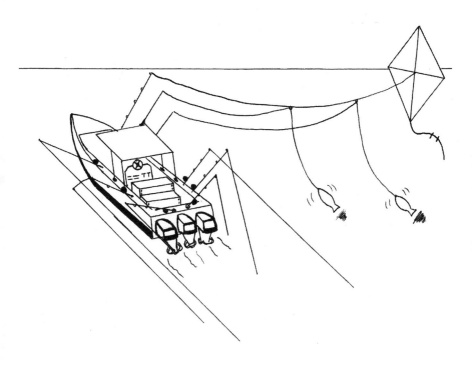

Large coverage kite rig includes 2 kite baits, 2 flat lines, and 2 downriggers. Flat line baits are used with the weights to keep them under the surface. This set-up is most useful along rips and drop-offs, or over wrecks and reefs. The kits allow a perfect position for the strike zone. This set-up is especially effective when trolling for Kings.

Spreader Bar Set (7/V Pattern)

Run the center bar closest to the boat.

V-pattern, Copying a school of bait.

75 – 100 Feet

Flat Lines

Transom Mount

Fish a single lure rig close to the center bar to imitate a weaker member of the school.

75 – 100 Feet

Flat Lines

Transom Mount

Outriggers

Center Rigger

Outriggers

Rig the flying fish on 36 inch mono terminal attached by a swivel.

Rig the squid on mono about 18 inches apart, five to seven squid, tipped off with the flying fish as the chaser.

Be sure each squid has a swivel and sinker on the lead end.

The chaser (flying fish) should be a few inches below the surface.

All of the squid should be the same distance apart and the same color.

The chaser should be further back and a different color to appear natural, thereby increasing the strike potential.

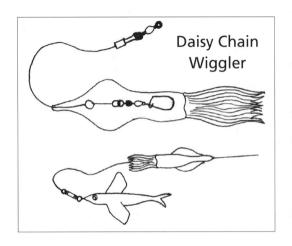

Daisy Chain Wiggler

Finding Deep Water Fish on Reefs, Ledges, and Flat Shell Bottoms

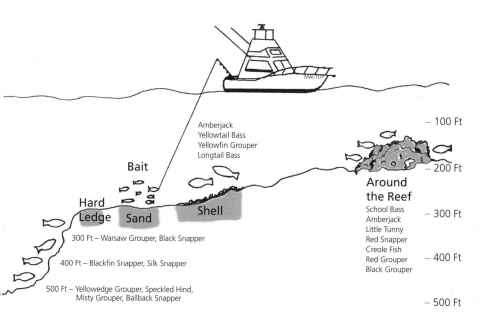

Amberjack
Yellowtail Bass
Yellowfin Grouper
Longtail Bass

Bait

Hard

Ledge   Sand   Shell

300 Ft – Warsaw Grouper, Black Snapper

400 Ft – Blackfin Snapper, Silk Snapper

500 Ft – Yellowedge Grouper, Speckled Hind,
Misty Grouper, Ballback Snapper

— 100 Ft

— 200 Ft

Around the Reef

School Bass
Amberjack
Little Tunny
Red Snapper
Creole Fish
Red Grouper
Black Grouper

— 300 Ft

— 400 Ft

— 500 Ft

Night Fishing
(the light method)

Using a light will attract the baitfish, which will then attract the predators. To begin, set up a fairly bright indirect light (one that spreads a wide view of light, much like a streetlight, but not as bright) at least 6 feet above the water. Turn the light on about one hour before the sun goes down; this will keep the baitfish from going into hiding and will lure them to your area.

You will notice a larger amount of bait being lured to the light over time. Once you have a school of bait, the bigger fish will move in. The bait will be in the brightest part of the light, while the predators will lurk far below where they feed along the bottom. Some top water fish may lurk around the dark edges of the light.

Once you've turned your area into the local hangout, your bait will be a crucial part of this fishing technique. Two variations are used, the 'injured baitfish' or the 'new guy in town.'

For the 'injured bait' method, you will need to use the same type of bait that is schooling, usually a type of minnow. Cut off one of the pectoral fins to make it swim abnormally and become an easy target for the predators. Drop your bait back in the middle of the action and let it swim freely.

The 'new guy in town' method is just as it sounds and will also catch the attention of the predators. Use a bait that is not included in your schooling fish. Find a spot outside of the light where you think there will be no predators. After your cast, lead it back to the center of the light and let it swim freely. This will not spook the predators and will give the appearance of a stray. If you are having no luck, injure the bait and repeat the same step for the stray.

For an added bonus, toss in some cut up chum.

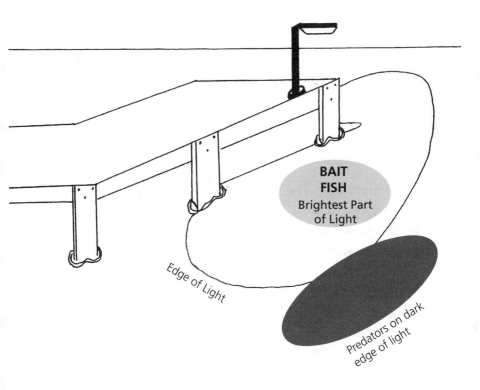

BAIT
FISH
Brightest Part
of Light

Edge of Light

Predators on dark
edge of light

Tactics for Catching Game & Sport Fish

In this section you will find an abundance of the highest quality fish pictures available today! I have arranged these pictures in a specific order that corresponds with my favorite fish. I enjoy catching some for their powerful runs and intriguing moves, and others for their extraordinary fight.

Before you view the rest of the book, I would like to clue you in on a few tactics used for catching game and sport fish.

HAPPY FISHING!

Snook

These fish can be found in many different conditions, and each requires a different fishing tactic as well as bait. Fishing for snook in rough beachside water (2-3 ft. waves) will require a deep diving lure to get under the surface. Top water plugs will work in these conditions, however, it is much harder to work the lure to the proper depth or proper retrieval, thus limiting your chances. In rough water many snook anglers say, " If you're not dragging the bottom, pack it up." To tell if you're getting the available action, make sure your lure is producing a steady back pull. If you feel your line become light, then heavy, you're probably skipping the surface or are caught in the underwash. Snook will come to the surface in rough water undercurrents, but would rather stay close to their shelter. When using live bait, free-line your bait so it will ride the current beneath the surface naturally. *REMEMBER, this tactic is for swift-moving rough water!*

Favorite Plugs
• Broken Back Long A Bombers
• Most dark green minnow lures (not top water)

Inland snook fishing takes on a whole new approach. Smaller lures are often more effective in shallow inland waters. Free-lining small pinfish near mangrove shores, docks, and seawalls has always produced great catches.

Toss a small pin near a sea wall and guide it back to you slowly – keeping off the bottom. This will tempt a snook resting nearby. Always keep your bait moving or it will often hide in the nearest shelter. Jigs tend to work well inland, provided you work them properly and start with a good jig.

In fact, I have had the best luck using a wild willy jig as my main bait around marinas. This method runs contrary to the notion that snook rarely hit your bait if they can see you, but this jig seems to change that theory. I walk the boat docks equipped with only my wild willy and 20 lb mono line. Find a good spot in 3-7 feet of water near a docked boat. Drop your bait in as far away as possible and bounce it off the bottom quickly and erratically. When it hits the bottom – repeat, repeat, and repeat. I have even had great results by tossing it in a few feet away where I can work it up and down in the same area. It will draw any nearby snook hiding under boats and resting the sea-walls. Try casting this jig on the grass flats and bouncing it back to you using the jerking tactics.

Cobia

Cobia are fish that can be seen schooling, creating head wakes that are visible from afar. To catch these fish you'll more than likely need to be in a boat or wade fishing for best results, but they are also found around bridges and piers. When scouting from a boat and you spot a school traveling across the flats, stay far ahead of them. Try to predict their path and drift quietly until the school is about 100 feet from your longest cast. Cast a small white bait or a worm body grub on either side of the path. Let your bait sit, occasionally jerking it as the school come near. Once the fish reach a distance of about 30-40 feet from your bait, begin a series of short quick jerks and one long – followed by a short rest on the bottom.

If you're using live bait, a float would be a good idea; be sure to keep the bait just inches from the bottom if in shallow water. Let your bait swim natu-rally. If in fairly deep water and you see a school, decide at what depth they seem to be and float your bait a few feet above or below that depth. Cobia like to strike up a hefty feeding frenzy, so be ready with a few lines. Keep one line in while reeling in the other, which will keep the school from moving on. Cobia also like to rest on the shady side of pilings in open waters. Toss a live bait beyond and slowly reel it past the opposite side.

Bottom fishing with cut mullet is also very effective. Put a nice size piece on a fairly heavy hook and drop it to the bottom, letting it sit. Position your cut mullet either on the edge of a channel, deep hole in shallow water, or the edge of a grass flat where the grass meets the sandy bottom. Cobia like to root out shrimp and crabs from the edge.

Favorite Baits
- Worm body grubs, and worms
- Live pinfish
- Cut mullet

King Mackerel

These fish run a few miles offshore when the water is cool. This fish is very fast and quick to take the bait. The most common way to work a school of Kings is to get out in the line of travel and troll with the same bait schooling in the area. You will have no problem fiding these fish if the run is nearby. The water will boil with hungry mackerel feeding on the bait run. You will see a long oil slick with birds diving in a frenzy. The mackerel rip the bait, leaving leftovers for other fish and birds. Drifting over shell bottom while free-lining a frisky live bait is also another method, but trolling seems to be the best way. Have plenty of bait and line, for you can assure a few cut lines. Toss in some dead bait here and there as you troll – this gives the injured bait effect.

Spanish Mackerel

Catching mackerel does not require much skill or knowledge on fishing. Basically, find out where the bait are and free-line one near the school. I have caught mackerel virtually everywhere I go. They run the deep channels, shallow channels and flats, and love to hang around piers and other objects which extend into the water. If you are in a boat, look for structures in the water that will provide baitfish cover from the predator fish and you will probably find mackerel. The best time to fish is when the water temperature is in the upper 60s to low 70s.

Redfish

Reds can be seen best during lower tides. Look for schools of redfish rooting out crabs and shrimp on the flats. You'll see their tails protruding from the water as they burrow their noses into the sandy bottom. Also look for oyster bars, as reds love to pick the bait from these plentiful sites. Reds must be stalked from a distance to get the best results. Drift into the area and anchor up as far away as possible. Cast a free-lined bait outside of the school and carefully work it into the area, giving the appearance of a stray bait. Do the same when using artificial bait. During high tides they can be found in abundance swimming the narrow channels of back water inlets, and around bridges where bait tend to pack up. Free-lining a shrimp near these bridges can be very effective. Live baits work best with these guys. Some jigs, like the hard body grub, are great in the mangroves.

Favorite Bait
• Hard body grubs
• Shrimp, crabs, and small white bait

Black Drum

This is a great heavyweight fish that pulls somewhat like a grouper. From land, fishing from a bridge will often produce the most drum – and the biggest! Winter and early spring is generally a good time to hook into one of these monsters. Use a good size hook (4-7/0) with a slab of cut mullet fully covering the hook. Rig your line for bottom fishing and drop in near or in the channel beneath the bridge. That's all there is to it, until you hook one! Theyu can also be found on or around oyster bars, rocky bottoms, and even in the surf. When fishing the oyster bars with cut bait, use the same method as bridge fishing, except cut back on the amount of bait and size of hook. If you wish to free-line a live bait, use the same method as if fishing for reds. When surf fishing, I like to use a float. The float rides the surf, causing the baitfish to flash as the surf pulls the float.

Seatrout

Generally an easy fish to catch. When the water is upper 60s to lower 70s, trout become full in the flats. If fishing from a boat, find a nice size grass flat about 3-6 feet deep and drift over the entire flat. Small lures and salty white baits work well. Greenback minnows are a favorite and should be free-lined on very light line. Cast out a lively minnow and reel it fairly slowly, being careful when setting the hook; if you pull too hard you'll rip the mouth of the trout. Small poppers and top water plugs work well. Trout bite best during moving tides when the bait are moving.

Sheepshead (see next section, p. 53)

Black Sea Bass

Mostly found around rocks and grass bottoms. Put the artificial bait away; these fish are dedicated to natural baits – cut or live. These fish are generally under 2 pounds, so use a small short shank hook with a small piece of choice bait. Rig your line for bottom fishing, using light tackle. When fishing live bait around rocks, secure the weight to the very bottom with the hook attached about 18 inches above on a 6 inch line off the main line. Use a 3 way swivel, connecting your standing line to the weight and your hook and 6 inch line to the swivel. Pull the slack from your line so the bait will swim in a restricted area without reaching the bottom.

Ladyfish

Ladyfish can be found most anywhere that bait is present. Free-lining a small pinfish over the flats or through the channels will drudge up a hungry lady. These fish fight much like a snook and offer a spectacular show if using light tackle. Shrimp is also a 'diamond' to the Ladyfish. Look for these fish anywhere near large bait schools – you will probably find tarpon and snook as well!

Tarpon

Smaller tarpon can be found far inshore around marinas, mangroves, and flats. The larger ones are often found swimming the channels near open water. To catch the smaller ones, free-line a pinfish as you would for a snook. Tarpon and Snook usually hang in the same areas inshore. Large jumbo shrimp will always tempt a tarpon. Remember, when you hook into a tarpon and it jumps to the surface to shake your hook, don't give it any slack or it's liable to

continued…

get away. To catch larger tarpon you'll need a nice frisky blue runner for bait, a strong hook (sized to the bait) and plenty of heavy line! You will not need to find the tarpon. When they are running you'll see many boats in a clustered in a small area. Slow trolling or still fishing are both effective. Mullet is also a great bait. For more information, see the tarpon entry in the following section.

Bluefish

A terror in the summer for northern waters, bluefish move south during winter months. These fish move across the bays ripping up everything in their path – even people, if you're in the way. They are ferocious feeders and can be caught by floating a live bait at mid-depth. Look for large schools working the surface baits. With bluefish, you can toss your bait into the middle of schooling bait and not spook the blue at all.

Bonefish

Bone fishing is a very popular event here in Florida. With the immense speed they possess, I catch the fever every year! Inshore bone fishing is a bit easier, for the smaller ones can be found running in schools over grass and mud flats, or back in the mangroves where they root for shellfish and shrimp. Set-up can consist of bottom rigs, free-lining, or floating your bait. Look for the moving school and present your bait in their path of travel. There's not much too it, but it's quite fun. Finding these guys may be your toughest challenge.

Snappers

Most snappers are the same and feeding habits are similar. My favorite way to catch snappers iw to free-line their favorite baits. Leaders are required for most snappers of size. Snappers are mainly bottom to mid-water feeders, but they will rise to the occasion. Cut bait will work for some of the species of snapper, but live bait is always better. If you are fishing in deep water, you'll probably have better luck using a weight to get your bait to the required feeding depth. For more information on snappers, see individual listings in the snapper section.

Flounders

One of the many unique fish with excellent camouflage, flounders can be found in mud, sand, and grass bottoms. They burrow into the bottom and wait for passing bait; they especially like crustaceans. Bottom fishing with greenback minnows or other small fish is the most common method. Flounder are often found where the water moves swiftly. Species such as the gulf flounder can be found hiding in the muddy bottom of tidal creeks.

Catfish

Anyone can catch a cat at any time and place. These fish eat anything and will bite on any set-up. They are hard pullers for their size and its strength will make you think you've caught a much bigger fish. Even though the fight may be a tug of war on light tackle, many consider it a nuisance, including myself. The Gafftopsail produces a very thick slime from its glands. If you happen to catch one, be sure to clean your hook and line well, as the slime seems to deter other fish.

Game & Sport Fish

See regulations on p.128 regarding these species.
*To view color illustrations, go to the Appendix listing
given under each fish name.*

• Common Snook
Color appendix D

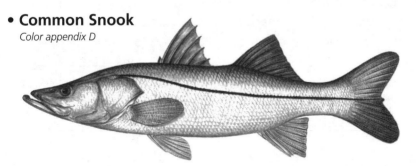

*Dark greenish-grey on back, shading to greenish-silver on sides
(above black lateral line). Black lateral line runs from top of gill cover to
center of tail. Silvery below lateral line, pelvic fin yellow.*

Value	Excellent
Size	To 45 lbs. in Florida.
Range	South Carolina and Texas, throughout Florida, Brazil.
Found	Grass flats, beaches, piers, bridges, warm water inlets (such as power plants).
Prey	Shrimp, pinfish, creek chubs, greenback minnows, and other baitfish.
Remarks	Snook are fast, powerful, and very intelligent. They are easily spooked. Chances are, if they see you they will not take your bait. They do not like water temperatures below 60° F. Heavy line or steel leaders may also spook them. They are very aggressive and prefer just about anything that moves on top of the water. Their gills are sharp enough to cut your line in two, and if given the chance will do this most every time.
Bait & Hook	When using live baitfish, size is of great importance. A palm size pinfish is probably the best size and a favorite for the snook. The palm size allows the smaller ones to take the bait, and also allows the big ones to swallow it faster. Therefore, when in close quarters you will be able to set the hook more quickly. Another good method is to blind the baitfish so that they swim almost non-stop, attracting the snook's attention. Snook love to prey on a fish in distress.
Handling	When handling a snook, never put your fingers in the gill sockets or the gill covers. Pick it up by the bottom lip using your first three fingers (thumb – middle). Your thumb goes on the inside of the mouth and others under the jaw. Keep the fish in an angle with his jaw locked open; this will prevent him from thrashing around as much.

Author's Tip:
*A common move for a snook is to come to the top of the water and try to shake the
hook. The best method is not to bow to him. If you bow to him, the line may get
behind the gill or he may shake the hook.*

• Cobia

Color appendix D

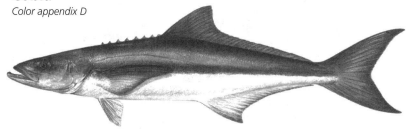

Mostly dark brown, white belly, Blackfish fins.
Dark stripe at mid-side, white stripe from snout tip to upper edge of
caudal fin, sharp spines forward of dorsal fin, flat head, protruding lower jaw.
7-9 free spines forward of dorsal fin.

Value	Good (slightly strong flesh)
Size	Average 15-30 lbs, up to 80 lbs.
Range	Massachusetts to Argentina; nearly worldwide in warm waters.
Found	Grass flats, wrecks, buoys, pilings, channel markers near or inshore.
Prey	Pinfish, grunts, greenbacks, shrimp, crabs, squid, deep-diving crank baits, jigs with worm body.

Remarks — Cobia are beefy fighters with a hard attack. They are one of our largest inshore game fish with some reaching 80 lbs. The largest recorded cobia was a huge 137 pounder. They are also the fastest growing inshore fish, reaching 80-90 lbs. in as few as 6 years. In the summer they can be found around wrecks, pilings, rotting structures, buoys, and even anchored boats. In the spring and fall they tend to roam the grass flats along with the reds and trout. In the winter months when the temperature drops, they move to warmer water, usually around power plants where discharge warms the surrounding water. They can also be found running with the stingray.

Bait & Hook — When using live baitfish, hook just slightly forward of the dorsal fin with a standard 3/0 straight eye hook. For other types of bait rigs, see baitfish section.

Handling — CAUTION: Sharp thorny spines forward of the dorsal fin can inflict serious pain and infection.

Author's Tip:
A good way to spot cobia is to look for moving water, dorsal fins protruding out of the water, running baitfish, or schools of stingray. Cast just ahead of the school and work your jig with a lot of action (if using artificial bait). Cobia are rather curious fish and once you have hooked one and begin bringing it in, the rest of the school will follow the hooked cobia wherever it may go. Have another line working the school and you'll be in the action for awhile. Another common trait for cobia happens when you set the hook. Cobia will turn head for a quick run and seem to almost give up while coming to the boat fairly easily. Just as you reach to grab him with a big smile on your face, he's back where he started and the fight begins to get remarkably harder!

• **King Mackerel**
Color appendix D

Darkish blue on back, fading to silver on the sides and a white belly.
Round dark spots with golden to yellow cast only in the young.
Front of dorsal fin is lighter in color than the second dorsal.

Value	Poor to good.
Size	Common to 20 lbs., but can reach 100 lbs. or more.
Range	Massachusetts and northern Gulf of Mexico to southern Brazil.
Found	Off Florida coasts, both near and offshore; occasionally taken from piers running into deep water.
Prey	Live frisky baits and trolled baits, also squid.
Remarks	A migratory fish found in the Gulf around spring and fall for a few weeks, then heads toward Northern waters. Also off of the Florida coast around March and late October throughout early November. They travel in large schools, taking vigorously to provided bait.
Bait & Hook	Free-line a frisky baitfish or blind the bait and cast into a school of other baitfish.

• **Spanish Mackerel**
Color appendix D

Dark bluish brown on back with golden spots above and below lateral line.
Silverish on belly.

Value	Oily but good.
Size	To 12 lbs. or 37 inches, average 2 lbs.
Range	Cape Cod to southern Florida and the entire Gulf of Mexico.
Found	Around bridges, channels, and flats. Northward in spring; returns to Southern waters when temperature drops to 70 degrees F.
Prey	Small live baitfish including shrimp and squid.
Remarks	Often confused with the young king mackerel, this fish produces a fiesty little fight and some intense speed. A very oily fish that is often used for chum, size permitting.
Bait & Hook	Small crank bait or free-lining a small baitfish or shrimp.

• Red Drum (known as Redfish)
Color appendix H

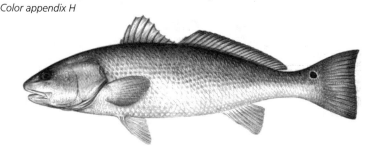

Larger ones are completely red shading to whitish red below with one or two black spots on base of tail. Younger ones are greyish on sides, changing to copperish red toward the back.

Value   Good
Size   To 95 lbs. Inshore up to 30 inches.
Range   Massachusetts to New Mexico, including Florida.
Found   Grass flats, channels, bridges, oyster beds. Spawns offshore.
Prey   Small fish and crustaceans, mollusks.

Remarks   A good game fish and a good fighter, prized by many fishermen to have
            high marks in all categories. They move with the inshore population to spawn.
            Large ones of 30 inches join spawning population offshore.

• Black Drum
Color appendix H

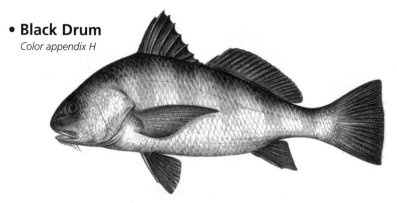

Dark grey or brassy with 5 broad black stripes.
Last one is shorter, stopping above lateral line.
Black fins, barbs on snout and chin.

Value   Fair
Size   To 100 lbs. or more.
Range   Nova Scotia (?) to northern Mexico, including Florida.
Found   Surf, bridges, piers, rocky bottoms, oyster bars; also offshore.
Prey   Live bait fish, cut bait, oysters, mussels, crabs, shrimp.

Remarks   A heavy puller and a strong fighter. When caught they make a loud
            grunting sound. Largest of Drum family, spawns near shore in winter and early
            spring.

• Weakfish (also Saltwater Trout)
Color appendix E

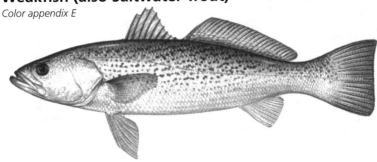

Dark olive to bluish above many dark small spots. Paler below with metallic reflections along sides. Yellow beneath and inside mouth.

Value	Good, but should be eaten soon after being caught.
Size	2 to 3 lbs., up to 10 pounds.
Range	Nova Scotia to Florida.
Found	Inshore bays in warm months and offshore in cooler months.
Prey	Minnows, shrimp, worm tail jigs.
Remarks	Looks somewhat like the sea trout except the spots on the weakfish are smaller and do not extend on the fins (opposite from the trout).

• Spotted Seatrout
Color appendix E

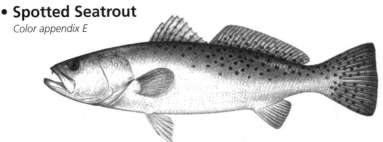

Bluish grey above, silvery to white below. Many black spots on upper side, 2nd dorsal fin, and caudal fin. Canine teeth on upper jaw.

Value	Excellent
Size	Average 1 to 2 lbs, but found to 15 lbs. or more.
Range	New York to southern Florida and the entire Gulf of Mexico.
Found	Grass flats, sandy bottoms, beaches, deeper water in winter (near shore).
Prey	Shrimp, greenback minnows, any little bait fish 1 to 2 in. (little pinfish work well), greenbacks are best.
Remarks	Some confuse the trout with the weakfish. Both are related and generally the same, but the trout has larger spots which extend up onto the fins; the weakfish does not. The seatrout has a comfort zone of 58° to 81° F.

Author's Tip:
When fishing in the flats, you want to go ahead of the flats and drift back over. Try to cast in the open sandy spots and reel over the grass. Don't retrieve too fast and be careful setting the hook, although the trout usually does it for you. Since their mouths are easily torn, slow retrieval from the mid-bottom works best.

• Sheepshead
Color appendix G

Sides are silvery to yellowish; back is dark olive brown with broad black bars across the nape; 5 to 6 slightly diagonal black bands cross the body.

Value	Good to excellent.
Size	2 to 3 lbs., up to 20 plus lbs.
Range	Nova Scotia and Gulf of Mexico to Brazil.
Found	Near pilings, docks, jetties, and wherever there are barnacles; also oyster beds.
Prey	Shellfish, fiddler crabs, and barnacles.
Remarks	These striped black and white fish are cherished by many old timers and anyone else able to catch one. Powerful and strong teeth make it hard to hook. It's one of the popular sport fish taken along the coastal waters.
Bait & Hook	Crack open a barnacle and carefully put the juicy treat on your hook; it falls off easily unless you've had some experience doing this.
Handling	Be careful of its mouth. The bite can be painful, as well as the sharp dorsal fin.

Author's Tip:
Throw down the poles and grab a spool of light line and a small hook. Use something to scrape barnacles from dock pilings; as the barnacles fall, the sheepshead usually come swimming over. Hang your line over your finger so you can feel the quick snap of your bait. Don't wait for a long tug – it won't happen. It will suck your hook clean in a matter of an eye blink.

• Black Sea Bass
Color appendix F

Head and body are bluish black to dark brown. The male is usually the darker of the two. The female is lighter with various blotches. The male has white to pale centers on its scales, and a white stripe on the dorsal fin.

Value	Good
Size	To 8 lbs. in southern Florida, average is 1.5 lbs.
Range	Maine to southern Florida and the Gulf of Mexico.
Found	Rock and grass bottoms, often in large groups around wrecks and fallen bridges, also in shallow water.
Prey	Barnicles, crabs, shrimp, small fish. Eats almost anything, cut or live.
Remarks	The average size is around 2 lbs. and under. They are quick to take the bait and give a series of little jerks when hooked. They are generally a soft, fleshy fish.
Bait & Hook	Basic tackle is a light rod and reel with a light hook and sinker rigged for bottom fishing.
Handling	Pull the hook out gently since they have a soft lower jaw. Be aware of the sharp spine near posterior margin of gill cover.

• Ladyfish
Color appendix E

Silvery all over with bluish or greenish reflections on body;
large mouth, small scales.

Value	Poor
Size	Up to 3 ft, average 2 to 3 lbs.
Range	Cape Cod (not common in north Hatteras); Bermuda, Gulf of Mexico and southern Brazil.
Found	Bays, channels, mangroves, and grass flats; spawns offshore.
Prey	Fish and crustaceans.
Remarks	This is a light tackle-buster with abilities of great speed and acrobatics. Fights like a game fish with great power; it is the cousin of the tarpon.

• Tarpon
Color appendix E

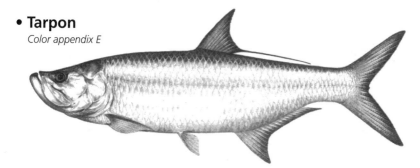

Silvery and dark greenish or bluish back.
Large mouth with protruding lower jaw; very scaly. Long filament at end of dorsal fin.

Value	Poor
Size	Average 40-50 lbs., but to 8 ft. and 300 lbs.
Range	Virginia to Bermuda and Gulf of Mexico to Brazil, also eastern Atlantic.
Found	Intracoastal waterways; spawns offshore.
Prey	Baitfish such as silver jenny, mullet, pigfish, and blue runners.
Remarks	A large and very powerful game fish that creates mass confusion among tarpon anglers who are fishing in close quarters or inlets. When hooked, tarpon will often run under other boats, possibly causing damage or accidents. A real treat to catch, but not to eat. Female lays more than 12 million eggs.

Author's Tip:
When you have hooked a tarpon, be sure to bow to him as he comes to the top of the water.

• **Bluefish**
Color appendix E

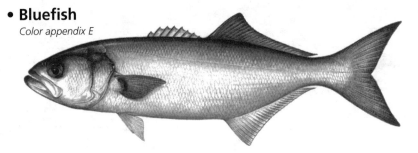

Greenish or bluish silver on sides with a blackish blotch at base of pectoral fin.
Second dorsal fin and anal fin are close in size and longer than the rest.

Value	Excellent
Size	To 25 lbs., average 3 to 10 lbs.
Range	Nova Scotia and Bermuda to Argentina. Rare between south Florida and Northern South America.
Found	Bays and estuaries. Young inshore during spring and summer, moving offshore to join adults in fall and winter.
Prey	Small baitfish, sardines, grunts, etc.
Remarks	Also called blue snapper, they migrate north in summer in large schools following the bait run. CAUTION: They have been known to bite anything in the water.

• **Bone Fish**
Color appendix D

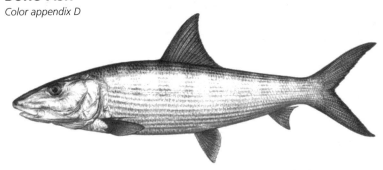

Polished silver sides and dark olive or bluish on back.
Dark streaks between scale rows on upper half of body.
Tip of snout blackish.

Value	Poor
Size	Rarely more than 10 lbs.
Range	New Brunswick, Bermuda to southern Brazil, throughout Florida.
Found	Mud and grass flats, also mangroves usually less than 1 foot deep.
Prey	Mollusks and crustaceans. Usually found rooting out shellfish, shrimp and fish from the bottom.
Remarks	Considered to be one of the fastest fish. Smaller fish often travel in schools, while larger ones are more solitary.

• **Palometa**
Color appendix G

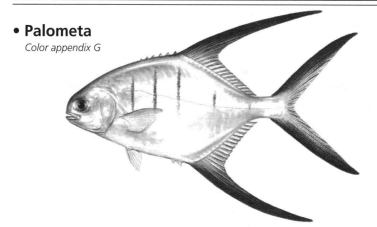

Bluish green on head and along back, silver on sides, yellow around breast.
Similar to the Florida pompano, except for front lobes of dorsal and anal fins
which are blackish and very elongated. Four narrow black or white bars on sides.

Value	Good
Size	To 20 inches, rarely over 1 lb.
Range	Massachusetts to Argentina, including the West Indies.
Found	Deep passes, shallow to moderate depths around reefs and surf zones; spawns offshore.
Prey	Top water minnows and crabs. Also takes well to small artificial lures.

• **Permit**
Color appendix G

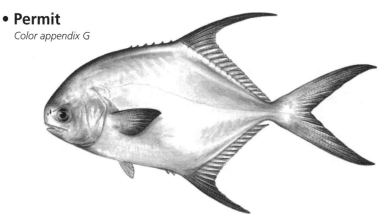

Blue or grey above shading to silver below.
Golden tinge near breast if from deeper waters.

Value	Fair.
Size	To 50 lbs, common to 25 lbs.
Range	Tropic and subtropic, mostly in the Florida Keys.
Found	Shallow flats and offshore deep waters.
Prey	Sand crabs, shrimp, clams, small fish.
Remarks	These fish are spooked easily and must be hunted with skill. Easily spotted by their dorsal fins protruding out of the water as they cross the flats in large schools, usually in a few inches of water.

• **Greater Amberjack**
Color appendix G

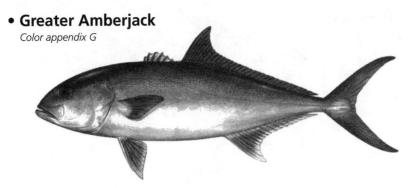

Mostly brownish above and whitish below.
Often have broad yellow stripes along mid-side in young.

Value   In some areas of the world may be poisonous; fleshy taste.
Size   To 176 lbs.
Range   Massachusetts to southeastern Brazil. Nearly worldwide in tropical waters.
Found   Around fishing boats, coral reefs, and open water.
Prey   Live fish and trolled baits, crustaceans.

Remarks   A very curious fish with little fear of man. May be found inspecting anchored boats or whatever else is in the area. The largest of the Jacks.

• **Crevalle Jack**
Color appendix G

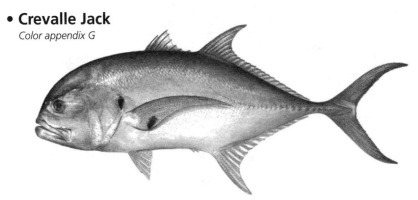

Steep slope on front of head, under parts and fins are yellowish.
Bluish-green to a goldish green on back and silvery yellow on belly.
Black spot on gill cover and base of pectoral fins.

Value   Fair
Size   To 20 lbs; Average 2 lbs.
Range   Nova Scotia and northern Gulf of Mexico to Uruguay.
Found   Bays, inlets, channels, open waters.
Prey   Any baitfish in the water, mainly small fish.

Remarks   This is the 'Tazmanian Devil' of fish. Always on the move in large schools. A very fiesty and hard-pulling fast fish.

• **Florida Pompano**
Color appendix G

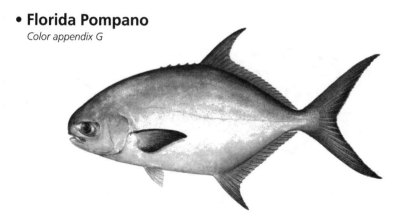

*Color varies depending on migration. If from the ocean, sides are
silvery white with light yellow fins. If from the river, they are darkened
to a paler yellow with occasional orange toned fins. Usually bluish on back.*

Value	Good
Size	1 to 2 lbs., occasionally to 8 lbs.
Range	Eastern seaboard (Massachusetts to southeastern Brazil).
Found	Near shore and occasionally inshore; oyster bars, beaches, inlets to offshore depths up to 130 feet.
Prey	Medium sized sand fleas are their favorite, but pompano also like shrimp and clams. For artificial bait, use a quarter ounce peanut jig tipped with shrimp. Various colored jigs include one with white, yellow, and pink heads.
Remarks	Known as a migratory fish traveling the entire eastern seaboard. Moving coastward from early November to mid-April. Best fishing around the coldest part of the year. As they move down the coast, some of the fish may move inland to feed on a large number of shrimp, crabs and clams that are plentiful on the flats. They are soft hitters much like a little snapper, but have a powerful zig-zagging run.
Bait & Hook	A basic rig consists of two #1 or 2/0 stainless steel kahlestyle hooks, one on a dropper loop and the other on the terminal end of leader. Use a 20 lb. mono leader with hooks approximately 10 inches apart below a small swivel. The entire leader should be about 36 inches long. Use a half ounce to 2 ounce slip style sinker on standing line.

• **Dolphin**
Color appendix F

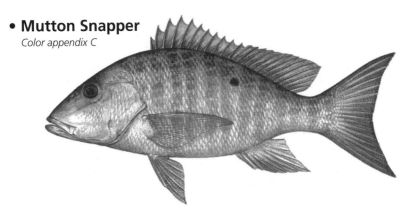

*Males are bluish-gold while females are greenish-gold.
The color will change quite often. Dorsal fin covers most of
the back, pronounced slant on head.*

Value	Fair to good.
Size	Average 30-40 lbs., often to 80 lbs.
Range	Nova Scotia to southeast Brazil; worldwide in tropical, temperate waters.
Found	Offshore open waters.
Prey	Live active bait fish (flying fish is best), and squid.
Remarks	A very beautiful fish with lightning speed, estimated to 50 knots. Flashes purple and various other colors.

• **Mutton Snapper**
Color appendix C

*Olive green on back and upper sides, overall orange-red in color.
Black spot on side of back near dorsal. Blue streak from eye to nostril.
V-shaped tooth patch on roof of mouth.*

Value	Excellent
Size	To 30 lbs, common to 15 lbs.
Range	Massachusetts, Bermuda, and the northern Gulf of Mexico to Brazil.
Found	Offshore reefs, mainly inshore around grass beds, mangroves, and canals.
Prey	Live and cut baits, snails, and crabs.
Remarks	Mostly caught while still fishing over reefs as bait passes by. Often sold as red snapper.

• **Gray Snapper**
Color appendix C

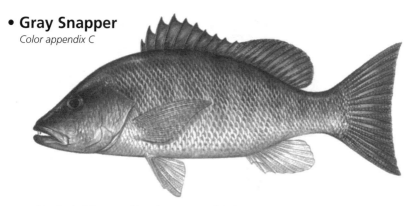

Usually dark brown with red tones. Broad dark strip usually present from snout tip through eye toward dorsal fin. Dorsal fins often have dark borders; rounded anal fin.

Value	Excellent
Size	Less than 2 ft., average 8 to 10 lbs. offshore.
Range	Massachusetts to Bermuda, Gulf of Mexico to southeastern Brazil.
Found	Young found mostly inshore around mangrove islands; offshore around reefs. Adults found near shore or offshore on coral or rocky reefs.
Remarks	Also called 'mangrove snapper.'

• **Lane Snapper**
Color appendix C

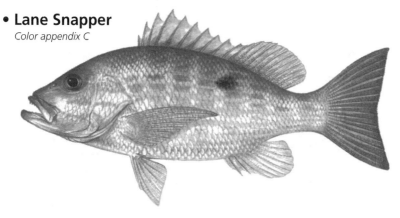

Large round dark spot on side. Silvery pink upper body, silvery below, and yellow stripes on the side. Pectoral, pelvic, and anal fins are yellowish.

Value	Good
Size	Up to 14 in., average 1 lb.
Range	North Carolina, Bermuda, Gulf of Mexico to southeastern Brazil.
Found	Shallow water around other shore fish, river mouths, inlets. Adults at offshore reefs.
Prey	Shrimp, small fish, mollusks. Mainly feeds on bottom.
Remarks	Very seldom found in schools. This is the smallest of the snapper family.

• Schoolmaster
Color appendix H

Greyish olive or red tones on back, fading to orange or white cast below.
Pale vertical bars from back to lower sides. Blue stripe below eye.

Value	Good to excellent.
Size	24 in. up to 10 lbs., average 3 lbs.
Range	Massachusetts, Bermuda, and northern Gulf of Mexico to Brazil.
Found	On bottoms and reefs among grouper; young on grass flats near shore.
Prey	Grunt, pinfish, and crustaceans.
Remarks	Considered one of the most attractive in the snapper family. These fish are abundant among the reefs and are usually found in schools alongside the grouper.

• Yellowtail Snapper
Color appendix C

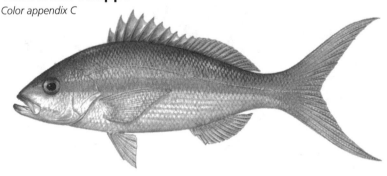

Light colored greyish blue , yellow spots and lines on upper side,
broad yellow stripe from snout to tail. Lower sides and belly have pink or yellow stripes.

Value	Fair
Size	1 lb., occasionally to 6 lbs.
Range	Throughout Florida.
Found	In medium depths, inlets, channels, and lagoons or offshore sand bottoms.
Prey	Small fish, shrimp, and crabs.
Remarks	A fairly good fighter that will take to almost anything as long as it looks to be alive.

• Scamp
Color appendix F

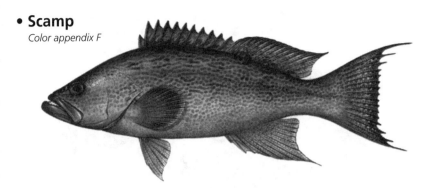

*Light grey or brown. Dark reddish-brown spots covering body,
grouped in blotches or lines.*

Value	Excellent
Size	10 lbs. and up to 24 in., Florida record 28 lbs.
Range	Massachusetts, northern Gulf of Mexico to Venezuela.
Found	Reefs and rocky bottoms.
Prey	Live white baits and crustaceans, also squid.
Remarks	It's not the size that counts, it's the quality. Considered to be one of the best in the grouper family.

• Southern Kingfish
Color appendix E

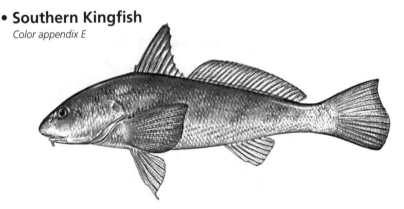

*Greyish blue silvery sides, up to 7 or 8 diagonal dusky bands or
blotches on each side.*

Value	Good
Size	Up to 15 in. and 3 lbs.
Range	New York to Texas, Bay of Campeche to Argentina.
Found	Shallow coastal waters, long beaches.
Prey	Live bait fish and crustaceans.
Remarks	More dominant than the northern king.

• **Gulf Flounder**

Color appendix F

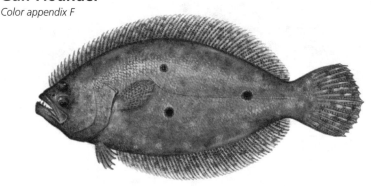

Brownish in color, 3 dark ringed spots forming a triangle.
Will change color depending on the bottom. Strong canine teeth.

Value	Good to excellent.
Size	Average 10-12 inches, up to 15 inches.
Found	Mud flats and rivers, sandy bottoms, and tidal creeks.
Prey	Crustaceans and small fish.
Remarks	Hatches into usual form, then right eye grows over to the left side. A bottom dweller that blends into its surroundings.

• **Jewfish**

Color appendix H

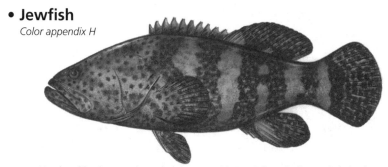

Head and body are pale to dark brown with 4 or 5 broad, diagonal darker brown
bars arranged in an irregular fashion. Blackish brown spots on head and fins.

Value	Totally protected from harvest.
Size	Average 20 lbs., often to 100 lbs., and known to exceed 750 lbs.
Range	Bermuda, Gulf of Mexico to southeastern Brazil, also the south Pacific.
Found	Deep holes around wrecks, pilings and cuts, usually in less than 100 feet of water.
Prey	Live baitfish, shrimp, and squid.
Remarks	Try to pull your anchor up in a swift tide with only your rod and reel. Hard? Well, that's basically the challenge you're in for when you hook up with one of these muscle fish. They are quick, but rather than using speed, they use a little ingenuity and wedge themselves into a hole in the rocks or reefs.

• Tripletail
Color appendix H

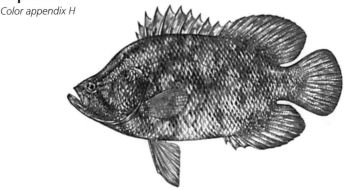

Head and body are tan to dark brown, with two dark streaks on top of the head, behind the nostrils. Fins are almost black, except for dorsal and pectoral.

Value   Good (not much meat).
Size   To 42 inches.
Range   Massachusetts to Uruguay. African Mediterranean and southern Europe.
Found   Open water, sometimes around wrecks.
Prey   Shrimp, crabs, white baits.

• Gafftopsail Catfish
Color appendix H

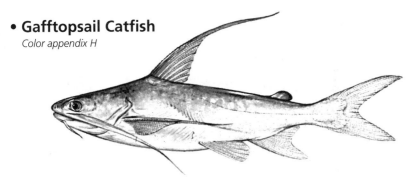

Bluish grey above, silvery below. Long pectoral fins.

Value   Fair to good (skin before cooking).
Size   Average 4 lbs.
Range   Massachusetts and northern Gulf of Mexico to Venezuela.
Found   Shallow to mid bottoms, sandbars, channels.
Prey   Live or cut baits.

Remarks   A fairly good fish with a bad rep because of its cousin, the hardhead. The Gafftopsail cat delivers a strong hit with an intense fight until the end. A real powerhouse!

Handling   CAUTION: Fins have a pointy spine and can produce an irritating infection.

• Hardhead Catfish
Color appendix H

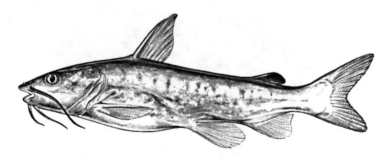

Brownish to grey-green above, white to yellowish below.
Barbs on corner of mouth.

Value   Not prized here.
Size   Average 1 lb.
Range   Throughout fresh and saltwater.
Prey   Live or cut bait.

Remarks   A hard puller for its size. Often a nuisance to many fishermen because they will
            eat anything.

• Swordfish
Color appendix F

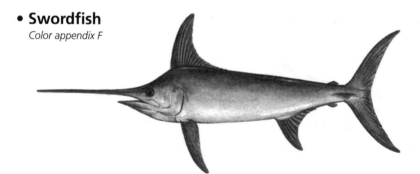

Body is dark bluish-green above and paler below.
No bars or spots; no teeth or scales.

Value   Excellent
Size   1200 lbs. plus, average 150 lbs.
Range   Mostly along eastern coast of Nova Scotia to Cuba.
Found   Tropical waters worldwide in about 600 to 2000 feet of water; comes to
            surface in warm, temperate waters.
Prey   Squid, octopus, and fish.

Remarks   Delivers fast, powerful runs – often leaping great distances out of the water.

• **White Marlin**
Color appendix F

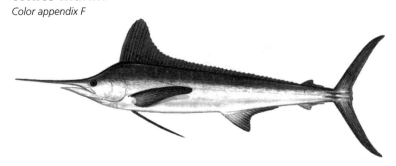

Similar to blue marlin, but lighter in color and is more greenish or dark brown rather than blue.

Value	Good
Size	Up to 180 lbs. (rarely), common to 8 feet.
Range	Same as blue marlin.
Found	Warm temperate waters of the Atlantic.
Prey	Pelagic fish and squid.
Remarks	Similar to blue marlin, but are much more acrobatic. Uses its bill to stun fish when feeding.

• **Great Barracuda**
Color appendix D

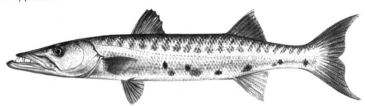

Dark grey on back, often appearing smoky black.
Actual color is a greenish cast fading to whitish below.
Pronounced spots on sides, spots are silvery below lateral line.

Value	None. Known to cause poisoning if eaten.
Size	6-7 ft. and 100 or more lbs.
Range	Massachusetts to southeastern Brazil. Nearly worldwide in warm temperate waters.
Found	Young barracuda in inshore grass beds, adults in inshore channels, reefs, and grass beds.
Remarks	Most attacks on man are due to spear fishing or causing a commotion. These fish will attack out of pure meanness and are very territorial. Seems to be attracted by shiny objects. Flesh is usually toxic in adults.

• **Wahoo**
Color appendix D

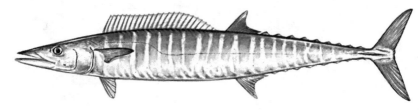

*Upper sides are dark greenish or a steel blue changing to paler silver, dark fins.
Yellowish bands run down from back.*

Value	Fair to good.
Size	15-20 lbs. average, to 180 lbs.
Found	Open waters.
Prey	Mostly caught on artificial bait by trolling.
Remarks	Known to be the fastest swimming fish in the water. Mostly travels solo; it shifts in direction when it's hooked.

• Little Tunny
Color appendix E

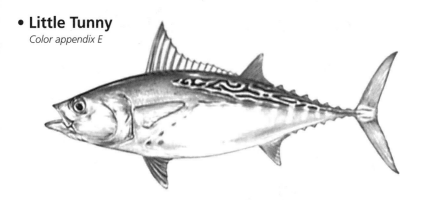

Bluish above with a silver belly and several wavy lines. Irregular blotches below the pectoral fin. 4 to 5 spots below pectoral fins.

Value	Good
Size	6 to 8 lbs., up to 30 lbs.
Range	New England to Brazil, most common in Florida waters during summer and fall.
Found	Inshore and bays, usually in schools.
Prey	Trolled bait, live baitfish.
Remarks	Indeed the most common tuna in the western Atlantic. Also used as a bait for marlin. Usually found in large schools offshore and in smaller schools inshore.

Less Abundant Fish Species

• African Pompano

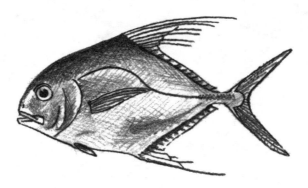

Silvery body with bluish green above very long filiform rays at the front of the dorsal and anal fins. Front of head is steep and rounded. Rear half of body is triangular in shape. Dorsal fin may exceed body length.

• Bluefin Tuna

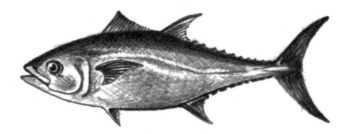

Bluish upper shading to white-silver below; Bluish fins; Yellowish tint on anal and second dorsal fin; Sizes to 1500 lbs. and 15 feet long; Ranges from southern Labrador and northern Gulf of Mexico to northern Brazil; nearly worldwide in tropical waters.

• Blackfin Tuna

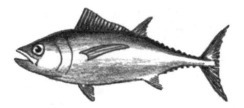

Goldish black shading upward to a darkish black on back; Sides are mostly white-silver; Fins are black with yellowish tints; Sizes to 40 lbs. or more; Ranges from Massachusetts and northern Gulf of Mexico to south Brazil.

• Caesar Grunt

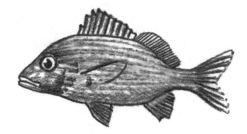

Body pale, often silvery with many horizontal bronze stripes; Dark head; Sizes to 14 inches; Ranges from Bermuda to southern Florida, Bahamas, and Yucatan to Brazil.

• Chub Mackerel

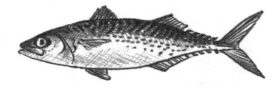

Bluish or greenish above, with about 30 wavy black bars across the body that break into spots toward base of tail; Sizes to 2 lbs.; Ranges from Gulf of St. Lawrence to Florida Keys and Cuba, nearly worldwide.

• Creole Fish

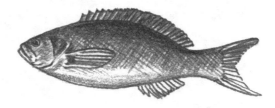

Dark red to brownish above, to a pale red below; May be olive in tone; Reaching sizes to 15 inches; Ranges from Bermuda to southern Florida and northern Gulf of Mexico to Brazil.

• Graysby

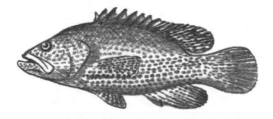

Four black of white spots along base of dorsal fin; Head and body may vary from pale grey to dark brown; Reaching sizes to 12 inches; Ranges from Bermuda to Florida and Bahamas, northern Gulf of Mexico to southeastern Brazil; Found on coral reefs.

• Northern Kingfish

Dark blotches running down and forward, one on the front of the dorsal fin forming a v-shaped pattern. Sizes to 18 inches. Ranges from Massachusetts to southern Florida, Gulf of Mexico to Yucatan. Found in shallow coastal waters.

• Rainbow Runner

Greenish blue above series of stripes on sides:
1) Broad dark blue stripe from snout to caudal fin base;
2) Narrow pale blue stripe immediately below dark blue stripe;
3) Broad yellow stripe along midside;
4) Another narrow pale blue stripe.
Whitish to yellow below, slender body. Sizes to 25 pounds. Ranging from Massachusetts to northern Gulf of Mexico to Venezuela; worldwide in tropical waters. Found in open waters, mainly in the Pacific.

• Red Hind

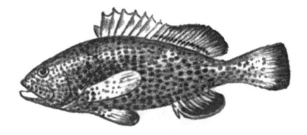

Reddish brown with dark spots. Spots on belly are pure red. Sizes reaching 2 feet, though usually less than 15 inches. Ranges from the Gulf of Mexico to the Atlantic, in fairly deep water around reefs. Eats live baits and crustaceans; regarded by many as a treasure.

• Rock Hind

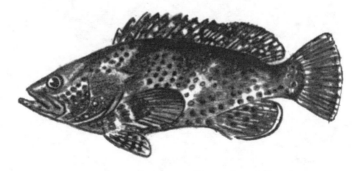

Tan to olive brown, with large brownish red spots that become larger toward the belly. Two or more rectangular blackish saddles on the back. Sizes up to 2 feet; ranges from Massachusetts to Bermuda and northern Gulf of Mexico to southeastern Brazil and eastern Atlantic. Found mostly around reefs. Eats live bait fish and crustaceans.

• Skipjack Tuna

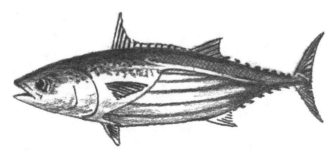

Belly and sides have 3-5 black stripes; Dark bluish on back; Sizes to 75 lbs.; Ranges from southern Nova Scotia and northern Gulf of Mexico to southern Brazil, worldwide in tropical oceans.

• Southern Flounder

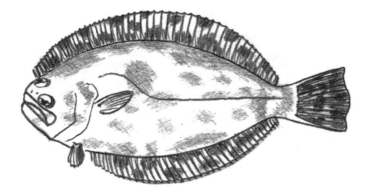

Often spotted and blotchy, relatively slender. Similar to the Gulf flounder, minus the spots.

• Tiger Grouper

Grey to dark brown or blackish; Inner mouth is orange toned; Reaching sizes to 20 lbs.; Ranges from Bermuda to southern Florida and Bay of Campeche to Brazil.

• Tomtate

White or pale tan with silvery reflections; Two bronze or yellowish stripes on sides; A dark spot at base of tail; Reaches sizes up to 10 inches; Ranges from Massachusetts to Bermuda, and northern Gulf of Mexico to Brazil.

• Vermilion Snapper

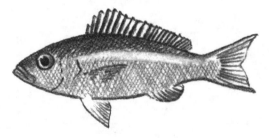

Entirely pale red, changing to silver below; Many short diagonal rows of blue spots on upper half; Sizes to 30 inches; Ranges from South Carolina to Bermuda and northern Gulf of Mexico to southeastern Brazil; Marketed as Red Snapper.

• Yellowedge Grouper

Pale grey or tan with yellow edge on dorsal, anal, and pectoral fins; Reaching sizes to 30 inches; Ranges from Florida and northern Gulf of Mexico to Brazil; found on rocky ledges or sea mounts.

• Yellowfin Bass

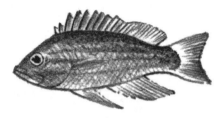

Pale red to orange-red; 3 or 4 broad yellow stripes on sides; White belly; Reaching sizes to 10 inches; Ranges from Virginia to southern Florida and the Caribbean.

• Yellowfin Tuna

Bluish-green on upper back, changing to yellow and becoming whiter yellow on the belly. All fins except first dorsal and tail are yellow; Reaching sizes to 400 lbs.; Ranging from southern Nova Scotia and northern Gulf of Mexico to southern Brazil. Worldwide in tropics.

• Yellow Jack

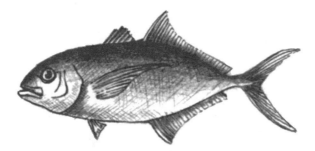

Dark yellowish above lateral line, paler shading below. Yellowish underparts. Sizes to 17 pounds. Ranges from Massachusetts and Gulf of Mexico to Brazil. Found inshore and offshore; feeds on baitfish and crustaceans.

Guide to Unique Fish

• American Eel

Value	Good
Size	Average 18 inches, but also to 48 inches.
Range	Fresh water, but they go thousands of miles into the ocean to spawn and die. The spawn go back to fresh water to complete the cycle.

• Atlantic Needlefish

Value	None
Size	Average 24 inches.
Range	Maine to Brazil, also in Gulf of Mexico.

• Atlantic Saury

Value	None
Size	To 20 inches.
Range	Worldwide in temperate waters.

• Bluespotted Cornetfish

Value   None
Size   To 6 feet.
Range   Occasionally as far north as Nova Scotia, worldwide in warm tropical waters.

• Houndfish

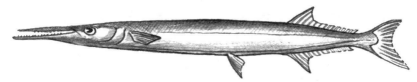

Value   None
Size   To 5 feet.
Range   As far north as New Jersey. Usually in southern waters.
CAUTION   *Can be dangerous to small boat fishermen. Has solid body with short sharp teeth and strong beak.*

• Trumpetfish

Value   None
Size   To 3 feet.
Range   Southern waters.

• Shortnose Batfish

Value	None
Fact	This fish comes complete with its own fishing tackle. A projection from its mouth lures in small fish.

• Atlantic Midshipman

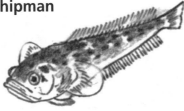

Value	None
Size	Average 6 inches.
Range	Tropical (common on Florida's west coast).

• Striped Burrfish

Value	None
Size	12 inches.
Range	Maine, Nova Scotia, northern Gulf of Mexico to Brazil on sea grass beds.

• Banded Jawfish

Value	None
Size	To 8 inches.
Range	South Florida to Bahamas to northern South America.

• Bighead Sea Robin

Value	Delicacy to some.
Size	14 inches.
Range	North Carolina to Gulf of Mexico and southern Florida to Texas.

• Smooth Head Scorpionfish

Value	None
Size	5 inches.
Range	North Carolina and Gulf of Mexico to Brazil.

• Beaugregory

Value	None
Size	To 4 inches.
Range	Maine, Bermuda and Gulf of Mexico to Brazil, eastern Atlantic.

• Blue Parrotfish

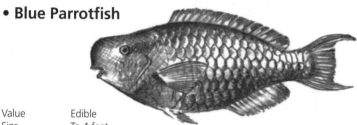

Value	Edible
Size	To 4 feet.
Range	As far north as Chesapeake Bay, but usually southern waters.

• **Butterfish**

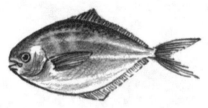

Value	Good
Size	Up to 12 inches.
Range	Eastern Newfoundland, Gulf of St. Lawrence, eastern Florida to Palm Beach.

• **Doctorfish**

Value	None
Size	Average 10 inches.
Range	Massachusetts, Bermuda, Gulf of Mexico to Brazil, also tropical west Africa.
CAUTION	*They have a razor sharp spine on each side of their tail.*

• **Lookdown**

Value	Oily flesh.
Size	To 12 inches.
Range	Maine to Uruguay and eastern Atlantic

• Atlantic Spadefish

Value   Fair
Size   Average 3 lbs., but can reach 20 lbs.
Range   Gulf of Mexico to southeastern Brazil.

• Jackknife Fish

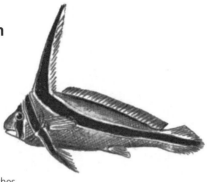

Value   None
Size   To 10 inches.
Range   North Carolina to Florida Keys, Bermuda, Gulf of Mexico to Brazil.

• Man-of-War Fish

Value   None
Size   Average 3 inches up to 10 inches.
Range   Worldwide in warm waters.
CAUTION *Usually found around the man-of-war fish-stinging jellyfish.*

• Queen Angelfish

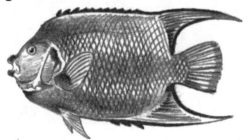

Value   Aquarium
Size   Up to 10 inches
Range   West Indies to Florida Keys.

• Queen Triggerfish

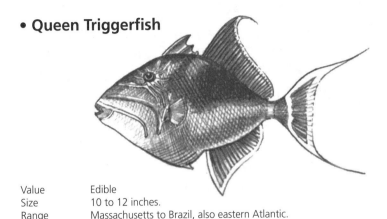

Value   Edible
Size   10 to 12 inches.
Range   Massachusetts to Brazil, also eastern Atlantic.

• Sergeant Major

Value   Edible
Size   To 7 inches.
Range   Rhode Island, northern Gulf of Mexico to Uruguay, nearly worldwide.

• Smooth Trunkfish

Value	Good
Size	10 to 12 inches.
Range	Massachusetts, Bermuda, northern Gulf of Mexico to Brazil, around coral.

• Southern Puffer

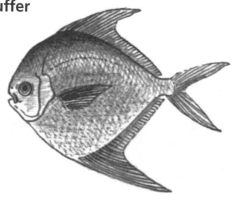

Value	Some are poisonous to some degree, but others are eaten as excellent food.
Size	10 inches.
Range	New England, Florida to northern Gulf of Mexico (east of the Mississippi), Bahamas to lesser Antilles.

• Spanish Hogfish

Value	Fair
Size	To 20 inches
Range	Bermuda and southern Florida, Gulf of Mexico to Brazil.

• Southern Stargazer

Value	None
Size	To 17.5 inches.
Range	North Carolina and Gulf of Mexico to Yucatan.

• Red Goat Fish

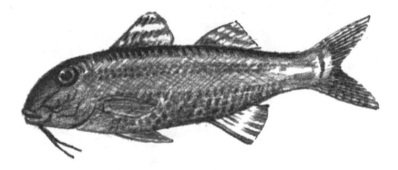

Value	Edible to good.
Size	To 10 inches.
Range	Nova Scotia, Bermuda to Guyana.

• Pilot Fish

Value	None
Fact	Often found around offshore sharks, giving the appearance of piloting them around. Has been observed to swim out and find the bait while swimming back and forth to bait and shark, as if leading the shark to the bait.

• Grass Porgy

Value   Good
Size   Seldom reaching 12 inches.
Range   Cape Hatteras throughout the south Atlantic and the Gulf of Mexico.

• Windowpane

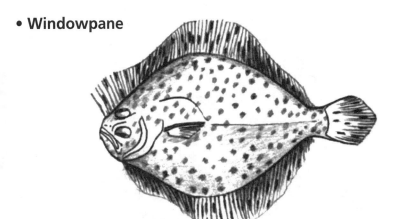

Value   Edible (boney).
Size   To 18 inches (very thin).
Range   Southern waters offshore, 150 ft. of water.

• Remora

Value   None
Size   To 12 inches.
Fact   This sticky-headed fish will catch a ride on any passing fish. Equipped with a vacuum cup on the top of its head that allows it to stick to other fish.

• Atlantic Stingray

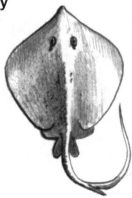

Value	Good
Size	Average 5 lbs.
Range	Throughout Atlantic and Gulf of Mexico.

• Atlantic Manta Ray

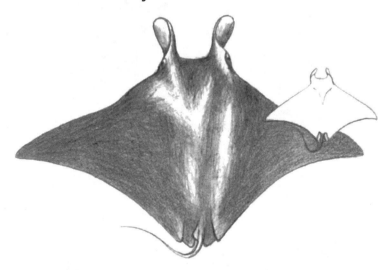

Value	None
Size	To 600 lbs. and more. Over a 10 ft. wing span. This giant creature is very gentle to man and feeds on plankton. Will often burst from the water turning flips.

• Spotted Eagle Ray

Value   None
Size   Average 150 lbs., up to 250 lbs. with a 7 ft. wing span.
Range   Mostly offshore deep waters.

Common Sharks of Florida

The myths and wonders of the shark world continue to attract our curiosity. Sharks are well-equipped fighting machines with a keen sense of smell – rightfully instilling a cautious fear of this so-called 'pit bull of the waters' into the minds of many.

Sharks use a variety of senses to scout out their prey, relying primarily on smell. They can detect blood in the water at levels as low as one part per million.

They also rely on their lateral line to detect the slightest abnormal motion in the water, such as vibrations, waves, and pressure changes from other swimming fish. One of the shark's most intriguing senses is a sort of built in sonar, known as the Ampullae of Lorenzini, used mainly for close range scanning. The ampullae are small gel-filled pits visible on and under the snout which detect the very instant that electrical fields are emitted from other living creatures.

Some may think that sharks are stupid because they have been known to bite on propellers of boats, floating metal debris, and underwater cameras among many other things. All of these objects carry electrical charges that confuse the shark into thinking he has a promising meal. Sharks will often bump into things since they don't see well and are merely testing what is unfamiliar to them.

Indeed, they are very diverse from any other creature, but should not be a reason to keep you from the water. The majority of shark bites occur from our lack of knowledge or sensitivity to their environment.

• Black Tip Shark

*Dark bluish grey above and white below. White stripe on flank.
Body is long and slender and the snout is equal to the
greatest width of the mouth. Black tips on fins.*

Size	Up to 8.5 feet.
Range	Massachusetts to the Gulf of Mexico and southern Brazil.
Found	Nearly worldwide in warm, temperate waters.
Remarks	Seen mostly offshore, but often enters into bays and inlets in large schools following the mackerel runs. Very popular on beaches. A fairly fast shark usually caught by fishermen in channels.

• Spinner Shark

*Dark bluish grey above and white below. White stripe on flank.
Snout is equal to greatest width of mouth.*

Size	Reaching sizes of up to 10 feet.
Range	North Carolina and northern Gulf of Mexico to Brazil, nearly worldwide in tropical waters.
Remarks	Often confused with the black tip shark due to both having black tips. Also known for its spectacular leaps and spinning moves when hooked.

• White Shark

Blue or lead grey above, fading to a dingy white below.
Dark blotches above pectoral fin. Large, heavy snout.

Size	Up to 26 feet, but usually less.
Range	From Nova Scotia to Newfoundland, and Gulf of Maine to northeast Florida and eastern Gulf of Mexico, also Brazil to Argentina.
Found	Usually with 3 or 4 of the same species.
Prey	Mostly large schools of fish.
Remarks	A sluggish species seen as not much threat to man; other family members, such as the grey nurse shark, are considered dangerous.

• Thresher Shark

Brownish to grey-brown above and a pale brown to white below.
Has a large eye, but smaller than the big-eye thresher.

Size	Up to 20 ft. and 1000 lbs.
Range	From Gulf of St. Lawrence and Nova Scotia to Florida; nearly worldwide in tropical and warm, temperate waters.
Found	Offshore.
Prey	Mainly fish and squid.

• Lemon Shark

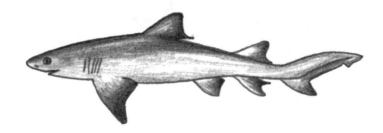

*Yellowish-brown to dark brown or dark grey;
olive on sides, paler below. A very short snout.*

Size   Up to 11 ft.
Range   North Carolina and Gulf of Mexico to Brazil, also west Africa.
Found   Coastal waters including bays and inlets.

CAUTION   A very dangerous shark, usually traveling in large schools.

• Blue Shark

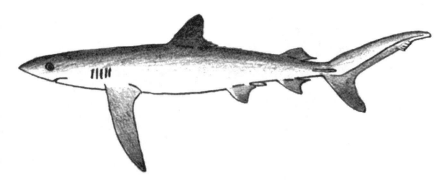

Bright blue above to white below; long pointed snout.

Size   Up to 21 feet.
Range   Nova Scotia to Argentina, also in Gulf of Mexico.
               Nearly worldwide in warm, temperate and tropical waters.
Prey   Mainly other fish.

CAUTION   A very dangerous shark, especially during maritime disasters.
               Will become very aggressive when a boat has gone down and people
               are in the water.

• Nurse Shark

Rusty or yellowish brown with a fleshy barb on the front of each nostril.

Size   Up to 10 feet, but usually less.
Range   Rhode Island (rarely), North Carolina to southern Brazil, also Florida.
Found   Shallow coastal waters from bays to outer reefs.
Prey   Mostly crustaceans and shellfish.

Remarks   Not much threat to man, but will bite if provoked. Small mouth on the
            underside with rows of crushing-type teeth. A sluggish fish that lies mostly on
            the bottom. In some countries, people ride these sharks like a horse –
            just for the fun of it!

• Bull Shark

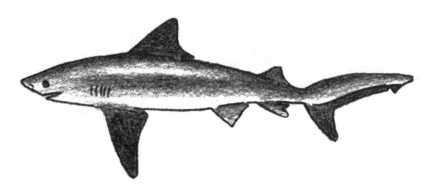

Grey to dull brown above, whitish below. Short and broad snout.

Size   Up to 11.5 feet.
Range   Southern New England to Brazil, nearly worldwide in coastal waters.
Found   Bays, rivers, tropical lakes. Rare offshore.

CAUTION   Very dangerous and known to attack man.

All four of the hammerhead species listed below are basically the same greyish to white in color.

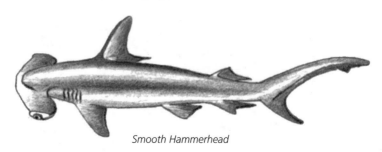

Smooth Hammerhead

Bonnethead

Great Hammerhead

Scalloped Hammerhead

• Great Hammerhead

Size   Up to 20 ft.
Range   North Carolina and Gulf of Mexico to Brazil, worldwide in tropical waters.
Found   Mostly offshore, but comes inshore to feed on stingrays, sometimes are as far inland as bays.

CAUTION   Very dangerous, mostly when the rays are inshore along the beaches in large schools.

• Smooth Hammerhead

Size   Up to 13 ft.
Range   Nova Scotia and New England to Florida Keys, Brazil to Argentina.
Found   Shallow coastal waters and bays.

CAUTION   Will attack when provoked.

• Bonnethead

Size   Up to 5 ft.
Range   New England and North Carolina to Argentina, also throughout Florida.
Found   Along shores and inlets to bays.

Remarks   Harmless to man and feeds mainly on crustaceans.
              Looks much like the hammerhead.

• Scalloped Hammerhead

Size   Up to 14 ft.
Range   New Jersey and northern Gulf of Mexico to Uruguay, nearly worldwide
              in tropical waters.
Found   Oceans, sometimes enters shallow waters.

Remarks   Very common in Florida.

• Sandbar Shark

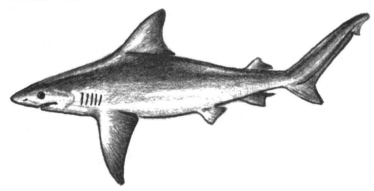

Dark grey to brown above, pale shading below. Has a short snout.

Size   Up to 10 ft.
Range   Massachusetts, Gulf of Mexico to southern Brazil, nearly worldwide in
              temperate and tropical waters.
Found   Muddy coastal waters and bays.

Remarks   A sluggish fish that migrates south in winter.

• Shortfin Mako

Dark blue back, white undersides. Very similar to white shark.

Size   Common to 6-8 feet, but sometimes to 12-14 feet and over 900 lbs.
Range   Cape Cod and Gulf of Mexico to Argentina. Mostly in tropical waters.
Found   Surface level in open waters offshore. Occasionally inland or near reefs.

Remarks   One of the most active and swift among sharks.

• Tiger Shark

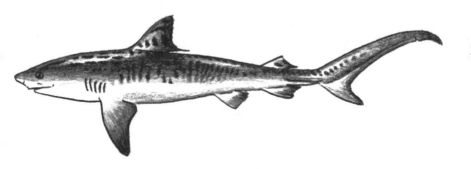

Dark bluish to brownish grey above, whitish below with dark spots and bars.
Has a short snout.

Size   Up to 24 ft.
Range   Cape Cod to Uruguay, most common from Florida throughout the Caribbean,
            worldwide in warm waters.
Found   Mostly deep water, but often enters shallow bays to feed.

Common Baitfish

• Scaled Sardine

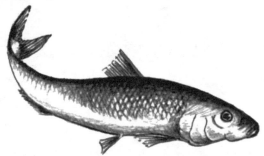

Silver on sides, grey on back. Belly is keel-shaped.
Found in saltwater, sometimes as far north as Cape Cod during warm weather.
Often caught using a ring set.

• Squirrelfish

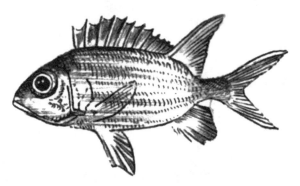

A reddish fish with large dark eyes. Found around offshore reefs at night.
A tropical fish that is great bait for grouper.

• Blue Runner

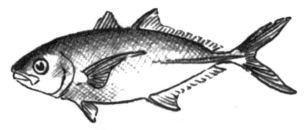

Greenish on back and upper sides, changing to yellowish silver or white; clearish fins.
Often dark olive to bluish above, and brassy below. Found around piers, marinas,
or in large schools of baitfish. Great shark and tarpon bait.

• Menhaden

Bluish upper with silverish brassy sides. Found in large numbers during summer along the Atlantic Coast. Great for chumming.

• Bay Anchovy

Olive colored with narrow silverish stripe.
Found around piers in inland waters, or in large schools throughout the Gulf.

• Inland Silversides

Greenish-blue on back, silver on sides.
Found in large schools around tropical and semi-tropical shores.

• Silver Jenny

Grey coloring beginning at the dorsal fin, changing into silver over the rest of the body, lighter on the belly. A humped back with a pointed snout found on shallow, sandy beaches or in brackish water. Good bait for snook and tarpon.

• Porkfish

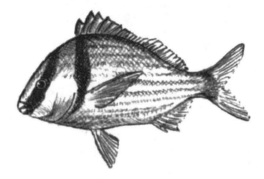

Two black vertical stripes on head. Body light-colored with overlaying orange toned horizontal stripes. Found around coral and rock bottoms. Mostly run in small schools.

• French Grunt

Grey-blue base color with overlaying yellowish horizontal stripes. Bright yellow fins. Found around rocky bottoms and bridges. Excellent bait for most game fish. White grunts are more common and are equally great bait.

• Pigfish

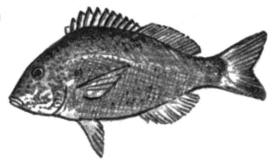

Light blue and silver striped, brown spots on snout.
Blue strip on sides of upper lip, inner mouth is whitish. Yellow tail with bronze
dorsal fin. Found onshore of Gulf and offers a great bait, especially for tarpon.

• Pinfish

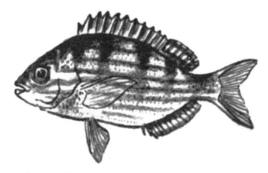

Black spot behind gill cover, a silverish grey with darker horizontal lines.
Found in grass flats, boat docks and ramps. Great bait for tarpon,
grouper, snook, and many more.

• Striped Mullet

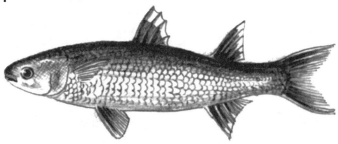

There are about 100 different species of mullet, most abundant in Florida.
Must be netted. Found just about anywhere in tropical waters and rivers.
A very oily fish; they mostly swim at the surface with their head just
slightly out of the water.

Quick Guide to What Fish Eat

Species   Prey

Albacore .... Live baitfish, shrimp.
Amberjack .... Live baitfish, mullet to grunts.

Barracuda .... Live baitfish of any species.
Bluefish .... Live baitfish, shrimp, cannibalistic.
Blue Runner .... Shrimp, small baitfish.
Bonefish .... Mollusks, crustaceans, fish.
Bonita, Atlantic .... Live baitfish, shrimp.

Catfish, Gafftopsail .... Live or cut bait (shrimp to pins).
Catfish, Hardhead .... Live or cut bait (shrimp to pins).
Cobia .... Small fish, jigs (worm body),
                                                           cut bait, squid, and crustaceans.
Coney .... Shrimp, cut bait.
Cottonwick .... Shrimp, cut bait.
Croaker, Atlantic .... Small live bait, cut bait.

Dolphin .... Live baitfish, shrimp, trolled baits.
Drum, Black .... Mussels, oysters, crabs,
                                                           small fish, crustaceans.
Drum, Red .... Mollusks, small fish, crustaceans.

Flounder, Ocellated .... Small fish, crustaceans.
Flounder, Gulf .... Small fish, crustaceans.
Flounder, Southern .... Small fish, crustaceans.

Gag .... Live fish, shrimp, squid.
Grouper, Black .... Live fish, shrimp, squid.
Grouper, Nassau .... Live fish, shrimp, squid.
Grouper, Red .... Live fish, shrimp, squid.
Grouper, Warsaw .... Live fish, shrimp, squid.
Grouper, Yellowfin .... Live fish, shrimp, squid.

Hind, Red .... Small baitfish, shrimp.
Hind, Rock .... Small baitfish, shrimp.

Jack, Crevalle .... Live frisky baits, jigs or lures.
Jack, Yellow .... Live frisky baits, jigs or lures.
Jewfish .... Live baitfish, other grouper, squid.

Species   Prey

Kingfish (Northern & Southern) .... Small fish, shrimp, trolled baits.

Ladyfish .... Shrimp, pinfish, other baitfish.
Leatherjacket .... All live baitfish, shrimp.

Mackerel, King & Spanish .... Small live baitfish, squid.
Margate .... Sand fleas, small crabs.
Marlin, Blue .... Live fish, trolled baits.

Palometa .... Top water minnows, crabs.
Perch, Sand & Silver .... Minnows, shrimp, cut bait.
Permit .... Sand crabs, live minnows.
Pompano, African & Florida .... Med. size sand fleas, clams.
Porgy, Grass .... Mollusks, shrimp.

Runner, Rainbow .... Small bait fish, shrimp, minnows.

Sailfish .... Live frisky fish, trolled baits.
Scamp .... Live baitfish, squid, crustaceans.
Schoolmaster .... Live baitfish, crustaceans, gastropods.
Seabass, Black .... Crabs, barnacles, shrimp, small fish.
Seatrout, Spotted .... Shrimp, small fish.
Shark .... Common bait
                                                             (cut mullet, stingray wings).
Sheepshead .... Shellfish, barnacles.
Snapper, Grey & Lane .... Minnows, small fish,
                                                             crustaceans.
Snapper, Mutton .... Squirrelfish, other fish, crustaceans.
Snapper, Red & Yellowtail .... Small fish, crabs, baitfish,
                                                             crustaceans.
Snook .... Silver Jenny, pinfish,
                                                             Greenback minnows, crustaceans.
Swordfish .... Large frisky fish, trolled baits.

Tarpon .... Pigfish, mullet, Silver Jenny,
                                                             blue runners.
Tripletail .... Crabs, small fish, shrimp.
Trout .... Minnows, shrimp, small bait fish.

Wahoo .... Live frisky baitfish, also trolled baits.
Weakfish .... Shrimp, small baitfish.

Hooking Your Bait

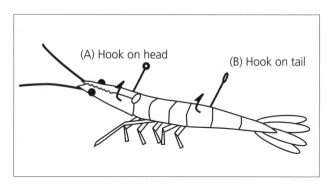

Hooking a **shrimp** differs, depending on the predator. Shrimp swim backwards when in danger. When using shrimp on any fish that swallows them whole, use the (B) position. For a fish that takes bites, like snapper, use the (A) position because the head is usually the first part to be snapped up in a chase.

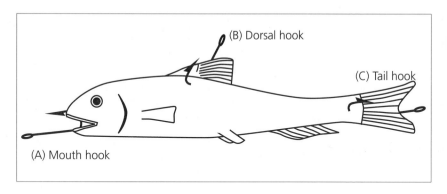

Minnows are commonly hooked as in this diagram, however, there are many other ways to hook them.

Position (A) can be used with a straight hook, or a quarter ounce to half ounce jig can be used in the same method.

When using a minnow as a crank bait, you will want to use (A). For free-swimming the minnow, use (C), and for bottom fishing with a weight, use (B). Also, (B) is used widely when fishing with a bobber.

There are many types of baitfish and many of them require a different hook placement. One single baitfish can have several ways of hooking.

Below are some of the most common ways of hooking baitfish in reference to their predators.

Note: Most baitfish can be hooked in all 3 positions for most predators.

Listed are the fish that need a specific hook position to encourage a successful bite. For example, when fishing for snook with a **pinfish** for bait, the best position is (B).

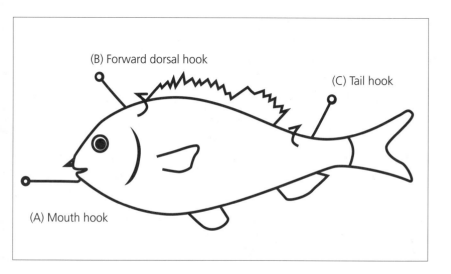

(B) Forward dorsal hook

(C) Tail hook

(A) Mouth hook

- **Cobia** – *all baitfish except minnows*   (B)
- **Snook** – *all baitfish except minnows*   (B)
- **Drum** – *all baitfish except minnows*   (B)
- **Large Snapper** – *all baitfish except minnows*   (B)
- **Grouper** – *all baitfish except minnows*   (B)

(B) is the best hook position for the above species.
If you are not sure about other fish, use the (B) position also.

Author's Tackle Box

It may seem considerably more difficult to use artificial bait instead of natural bait, but many anglers disagree. Each type of bait presents its own challenge in order to make it appear 'live.' When using artificial bait, you must take care to insure a lifelike action, but the benefit of using a lure is that fish will usually strike at it more quickly than live bait since there is less time to inspect and hit it. Seldom will a fish turn away from a lure that has been well presented. When it comes to natural bait, however, fish have more time to inspect the prey before taking it. For this reason, attention to detail is crucial. Your potential catch can be spooked by the slightest imperfection. The line could be visible, too much hook might be showing, or the hook might even be the wrong color. These are a few of anglers' most common mistakes.

On the following pages are some of the Author's favorite lures and jigs, along with their use.

My Favorite Lures

One of the hardest aspects of fishing is stocking your tackle box with the proper tackle. There are many different lures, jigs, and hooks to choose from and while most are similar in color and style, knowing how to pick the right one is a task for the average fisherman. When picking out a lure, I always look for those that look, react, and feel like the real thing. I have given a description of my favorite lures below to help you choose from the thousands available.

Snook

My favorite fish deserves the best lure I can find. This lure is a 'long A' hard body Bomber with a broken back for more action. It has a red head with rattling balls inside, white belly, and a clear body with a mirror like strip imbedded in the center to give it the flashy appearance. I use this large lure for the turbulent areas along the Gulf beaches. For areas inland, switch to a smaller lure of the same type.

Also, the 'wild willy' jig has earned its way into my box. It has a bright orange lima bean head with a yellow-haired tail; this jig has pulled many large snook from sea walls, beneath docked boats, and grass flats.

Trout

A favorite of mine in the smaller class of fish. I use a 2 inch split tail grub with a yellow body, 3 black spots on the belly. Use a small orange jig head. This little jig has pulled more trout for me than the traditional greenback minnow. This jig is very durable and most of all effective.

Cobia

This is truly a great fish to battle. I use a hooked tail grub with a white rattler jig head, 3 inches in length. The color will vary depending on weather conditions. I have the best luck by using the brighter baits to start out and switch to darker if they are not interested.

Spanish Mackerel

These fish love minnows and grubs, so I tend to stay with a similar jig bait. I use a greenback hook tail rubber with a white rattling jig head. As for grubs, I use a clear body grub with black and silver flash inside. Also, I have good luck with small rubber minnows, black on the back with bluish-silver sides. The sides look dingy white, but when you move it around it will flash the hidden color prism.

Redfish

I have caught reds on many of the lures and jigs mentioned above, but my favorite are the rubber minnows. I have had good luck on mainly two colors. The first one is mainly used in fresh water but has been an addition to my box for quite some time following a catch of 22.6 pounds from this little Cocahoe minnow. It has an orange head and a pure white body, approximately 5 inches in length with silver and gold flash inside; both have a thick beveled tail that produces great tail action. Grub tails are also effective.

Other fish

For other fish such as grouper and snapper, I use two jigs as my all around multi-purpose jigs. The wild willy mentioned above and the well known bullet head jigs.

Note

Lures and jigs are effective, however, I like to use live bait to start and switch to artificial if they are not taking the live bait. In my opinion, live bait will always be tops on my list, for this is their natural bait and it is impossible to create an exact replica.

Nearly all of the artificial bait available will work to some degree, but the most important aspect of artificial bait is presentation. If you are using a good bait but not in the proper way, the fish will see this and most often are spooked. Learn the proper methods for each bait that you use and you're sure to increase your catch.

Author's Tampa Bay Fishing Hot Spots

Knowing where the fish are makes fishing a lot easier and more productive. Below are some of my favorite spots throughout Tampa Bay, most between the Skyway and Gandy Bridges. On the St. Petersburg side between the two bridges are numerous long stretches of sand bars home to trout, reds, snook, shark, and many others. While most of these spots are good locations, particular ones stand out:

• Coffee Pot Bayou
Mostly around the bridge leading toward the boat ramps, and around the island, just east of the bridge.

• Weedon Island
This area has many hot spots back in the mangroves among the grass flats and oyster beds. Remember, there are no gas-powered engines allowed beyond the posted signs.

• Gandy Main Span
Off the west side heading north from the Skyway. There is a sunken boat that offers a variety of fish.

• Power Plant
Located next to the Gandy Bridge, it is an excellent place to fish during cold winters. The discharge from the plant warms the surrounding water, bringing in a lot of snook, cobia, and many others.

• Sand Bar from Gandy to Skyway
There is a long stretch of sand bar running from bridge to bridge, with occasional breaks for inlets. From the Coast Guard Base southward, there is always a wide variety of fish in this favorite spot that creates a smile everytime I visit. (continued...)

• Beer Can Island

Located on the Tampa side of the bay, Near Gandy and MacDill Air Force Base. The outskirts of the island and the tip of the sand bar are good spots during tidal movement. The tide rips past the island with strong currents and is best when fished from the opposite side of the tide. The fish tend to pack up in the calm area and wait for passing bait.

*See "Free-line the Structures," page 8.

• East Side of Skyway

There are waterways leading throughout the flats and mangrove shores. All through this area you will find trout, reds, snook, and more.

• Gulf of Mexico, between Egmont Key & Fort DeSoto

Out in this part of the Gulf the water ranges 45 to 75 feet throughout the channel. This is a good location to fish if you're looking for a variety of species.

Recipes

Poached Fish / *by the author*

You'll need:
- One fish of your choice over 5 lbs., cleaned, but with head & tail intact. Measure fish thickness in inches, side-to-side at its widest point. If using a smaller fish, reduce ingredients proportionately.
- One sliced lemon
- One sliced orange
- One sliced lime
- One tsp. salt
- 2 cups dry white wine

Use a fish poacher with a removable rack. Prepare the poaching liquid in the poacher by combining the 2 cups of white wine with 2 quarts of water. Add 3 or 4 slices of each fruit, along with the salt.

Slowly bring liquid to a boil, then reduce heat so that there is a slow yet constant motion on the surface. Continue to simmer for 15 minutes.

Slowly lower fish into the simmering liquid and cook for 10 minutes per inch of thickness. A 2 inch fish will cook for 20 minutes. Remove fish from the poacher, carefully lifting the rack. Serve with your favorite accompaniments.

This recipe is best when made with fresh Red Snapper.

Citrus Snapper / *by the author*

You'll need:
- Fillet of snapper
- 3/4 cup diced pineapple
- 1/4 cup lemon juice, or 1/2 lemon, peeled
- 1/2 seedless orange, peeled
- 1 Tbsp. olive oil
- 1 tsp. salt
- 5 Tbsp. butter

Combine all ingredients except snapper into a blender and blend to liquid form. Pour liquid into a fish poacher, slowly bring to a boil, then reduce heat so there is just a small constant motion on the surface. Simmer liquid without fish for about 5 minutes.

Lower fish into simmering liquid and cook for 10 minutes per inch of thickness. Fish should be completely submersed.

(If a poacher is not available, use tin foil layered a few times to form a pan shape and pour liquid to cover entire bottom).

Cook for 45 minutes on each side, keeping a layer of liquid on the bottom to insure flavoring. You may fill pan to higher level, but be careful that it doesn't run over. Occasionally baste the top of the fish with poaching liquid.

Marinated Fish / *Sammy Carter*

You'll Need:
- Fillet of fish, your choice
- Jar with lid
- Lemon juice
- Vinegar

Fill a jar with 60% vinegar and 35% water. Add in 5% lemon juice or your choice of flavoring, but lemon works with vinegar the best.

Put in raw fillet of fish and let it marinate for 4 days in the refrigerator. The vinegar will cook the fish, so there is no need for further cooking.

This recipe is widely used by those who acquire a taste for beer.

Sliced Marinated Fish / *Sami Z. Anani*

You'll Need:
- 2 lb. fish, gutted and sliced into quarters
- 2 Tbsp. ground cumin
- 2 heads garlic, finely crushed
- 3 fresh lemons, cut into 1 inch slices
- Flour and cooking oil

Mix seasoning, garlic, and lemon. Put into a saucepan and add fish until it it is covered inside and out. Let sit for 30 minutes. Heat cooking oil. Shake marinade from fish and immediately roll fish pieces in flour. Fry to a golden brown.

 * Tip: If grilling fish, use high heat just long enough to crystallize or brown the outside on both sides after you've marinated it. This will seal in the flavoring. Then return to medium or low heat and follow directions.

Fish Chowder / *Sammy Carter*

You'll Need:
- Onions
- Potatoes
- Celery
- 1 can cream of mushroom soup
- 1 can of condensed milk
- Fish

This recipe will be adjusted according to your taste and the amount you wish to make. Chop up desired amount of onions, potatoes, and celery; add to boiling water and cook until done, about 20 minutes. Drain water and pour in condensed milk and mushroom soup, mix well. Let simmer for 5 minutes without the fish, stirring 4 or 5 times.

Add fish and cook until fish is soft and flaky. Fish can be pre-cooked and simmered in sauce for 20 to 30 minutes. Add more mushroom soup for a thicker base.

Fish Burgers / *by Jeff Scott*

You'll need:
- 1 egg per pound of fish
- 1/3 cup of chopped onions, more or less to taste
- 1/4 tsp. garlic powder
- 1 tsp. Old Bay seasoning
- 1/3 cup thousand island dressing
- Bread crumbs

Microwave the onion for 1 1/2 minutes on high and set aside. Combine all the ingredients and mix to the texture of raw hamburger. Form into patties and spray lightly with oil. Grill until golden brown. Flaking may occur on a standard grill rack; if available, use a smaller size rack made for fine objects.

Puffed Beer Batter / *by the author*

Many of us enjoy a smooth puffed batter on fish, restaurant style. I have perfected this batter without costly store-bought ingredients.

You'll need:
• Flour
• Your favorite beer
• Lemon juice

Pour 1 cup flour and 3 tablespoons of lemon juice into a mixing bowl. Pour about 7 oz. of beer into a bowl and mix well into a liquid form.

Note: For a puffier crust, use less beer and mix into a sticky paste.

Coat the fish and fry on medium high or about 300 degrees until golden brown.

First Aid

The following first aid guide will be helpful in the unfortunate incident of a maritime medical call. This section was added to aid in the survival should a medical problem occur, minor or major, *HOWEVER, you should be aware of all the procedures before the incident arises and should take some basic courses annually to keep you current on the procedures.*

This section has been simplified by the author for faster response time and is only recommended in the event that the user is lacking medical knowledge and is in need of help. This section has been reviewed and approved by medical personnel, however, it is always best that you attend the many courses available to further your knowledge.

• Rescue Breathing (Mouth to Mouth Resuscitation)

To assess if rescue breathing is needed:
- Look at victim's chest to see if it's rising and falling
- Listen near mouth and nose for sounds of respiration
- Feel with your cheek for moving air from mouth or nose

IF NO RESPIRATION, CALL FOR HELP AND BEGIN RESCUE BREATHING

Steps to begin rescue breathing:

1) Lay victim on back on a firm surface.

2) Tilt the victim's head back using one hand under the neck, gently lifting up while the other hand is on the victim's forehead gently pushing down, securing the head to open the airway. Angle of head is important – too far back or not enough can restrict the airway. Adults need the greatest angle while children need less, and infants the least. *NOTE: If you suspect a neck injury, limit head tilt to a minimum; open the airway by lifting the jaw and holding the chin.*

3) With the hand you're using to keep victim's forehead at an angle, also pinch the nostrils closed using your thumb and forefinger.

4) Open the victim's mouth using your hand nearest the victim's feet.

5) Take a deep breath and give to victim; you are giving the correct amount of air if the victim's chest is rising fully when you exhale into victim's mouth. *NOTE: Infants require less air; be careful not to give too much air, as it can harm the infant.* If chest is not rising properly, check angle of head. If still having problem, check to see if a foreign object is lodged in the throat. Make sure your lips are fully covering the victim's mouth to ensure a good seal. If unable to seal the mouth properly, close victim's mouth and place your mouth over victim's nose and administer breathing. For infants, cover both mouth and nose with your mouth. For animals, seal the mouth closed with your hand and administer breathing through   nose.

6) If water or vomit begins to come out of the mouth, turn victim's head or body to the side and sweep out the debris, reposition them on their back and continue resuscitating. If you suspect a neck injury, roll victim's head head and back at the same time, keeping them in alignment.

7) Check for a pulse. An adult's pulse is in the neck, just to the side of midline. For infants, check pulse on inside of upper arm. Depress the area for 10 seconds using 2 fingers (NOT your thumb or you will be feeling your own pulse). If a pulse is present, continue giving rescue breathing at a rate of 1 slow breath every 5 seconds for adults, and every 3 seconds for children and infants.

8) Recheck pulse and breathing every 1-2 minutes. Continue breathing as long as pulse is present and victim is not breathing. If victim begins to breathe, end rescue breathing.

9) If victim's pulse stops, begin CPR.
   (CPR is necessary only if there is no pulse).

• CPR (Cardiopulmonary Resuscitation)

1) After two breaths are administered, begin chest compressions. Locate the sternum (breastbone) by following the curve of the ribs to the midline of chest. Measure 3 finger breadths up from that point and place the heel of your hand over the sternum. For infants, this is between the nipples. For children use only one hand, two for adults.

2) Keeping your elbows straight, apply pressure downward using your upper body weight as the compressing force.

3) Give 15 compressions followed by 2 breaths, if CPR administered by one person. If administered by 2 persons, give 5 compressions and 1 breath. Recheck for pulse and respiration every 1-2 minutes.

4) Compressions for infants should be approximately a half-inch using 2 fingers; compressions for children ages 1-8, 1 inch using 1 hand; Compressions for adults, 2 inches using 2 hands.

• Choking

CONSCIOUS CHOKING VICTIM

Assess if assistance is needed:
Ask, "Are you choking? Can you speak?" As long as the victim can cough forcefully, stay nearby and encourage his coughing effort. If the cough becomes weak or the victim can no longer breathe, give abdominal thrust.

Abdominal thrust method for conscious adults and children in standing or sitting position:
1) Stand behind the victim, wrapping your arms around them.

2) Make a fist with one hand, placing the thumb side of your fist against the victim's abdomen, just above the navel. Grasp your fist with your other hand.

3) Administer 5 forceful and rapid upward thrusts. Remove pressure between each thrust.

4) Repeat until the object is cleared or the victim becomes unconscious.

METHOD FOR INFANTS (CONSCIOUS OR UNCONSCIOUS)

1) Cradle the infant over your forearm face down with the head pointing down toward the floor.

2) Give the infant 5 blows on the back, between the shoulders.

3) Turn the infant over while balancing the infant on your arm. Give 5 half-inch deep chest compressions between the nipples.

4) Open infant's mouth and look for the object obstructing the airway. If you can see the object, try to remove it, but be careful not to push it further down.

METHOD FOR UNCONSCIOUS CHOKING VICTIM

1) Attempt rescue breathing as described on page 107.

2) If the air will not go in, place the heel of one hand against the middle of the abdomen, just above the navel. Place the other hand over the hand on the abdomen and give a forceful upward thrust.

3) Open the mouth and search for the obstructing object. If you see it, sweep it out carefully.

4) Tilt head again and try rescue breathing; continue until breaths can be given.

5) Once the object is removed, continue rescue breathing until victim is breathing spontaneously. If the victim's airway has been blocked for more than 1 minute, contact medical consultation immediately.

• Sun and Heat Exposure

When outside, it is always best to protect your skin from the sun even if the sun is behind the clouds – you can still get a burn. Wear a sunblock of Spf 15 or greater, a wide brimmed hat and some zinc oxide on those areas at greatest risk, such as the ears and nose.

Procedures:
Once sunburn has occurred, take special care to protect from further damaging rays and from poorly fitting clothes that may cause further irritation. Sunburn creams and ointments will help cool and moisturize the burned skin, but it is necessary to use a burn ointment if the skin is blistered. Drawing the heat from the skin will alleviate the pain and/or most of the swelling. If no blistering has occurred, take a cool shower (the longer the better), use moisturizer burn cream, gel or spray, take a pain reliever and use a cool compress to the worst areas of pain. Also keep your living quarters as cool as possible; this will aid in a speedy recovery.

Blistering will require an antibiotic ointment or cream with a sterile dressing covering the burned areas. Be sure to leave the blistered skin intact, however.

If the blister ruptures, this thin layer of skin may be gently removed with forceps and a new dressing applied. Change the dressing daily. A physician should be consulted if blistering or signs of infection occur.

• Heat Exhaustion and Heat Stroke

Heat exhaustion and heat stroke are caused when the body's core temperature is significantly elevated. It must be lowered immediately.

Procedures:
Moisten the skin with water and allow it to evaporate, continuing until the victim becomes stable or medical help arrives. Application of cool dressing or compresses applied to the body may also be beneficial. Be sure the compress or dressing is cool, not cold. Also be sure to keep the dressing or compress cool. If the victim is unconscious for more than 30 seconds or body temperature is greater than 104 degrees F, obtain medical attention immediately.

• Hypothermia

Hypothermia results from the loss of body heat, which occurs both on land and in water. If on land, the main course of action is to find whelter from the wind. Wool and synthetic clothing hold heat much better than other materials. Staying active, but not to the point of perspiration, will accelerate your body heat.

If in the water, the main course of action is to stay afloat. Keeping your head above water will help to hold in the heat. Keep your arms curled around the flotation device, legs crossed and bent at the knees, drawing them closely to your chest. This position will center the heat to the mid-section of your body and keep you insulated. Huddling with others will also help to slow heat loss.

Symptoms of hypothermia:
Shivering, muscle stiffness, slower heart rate, confusion – leading to unconsciousness. (continued…)

Procedures:
Remove victim from water, assess the airway, breathing, and circulation (A.B.C.). If victim has no pulse or respiration, begin CPR immediately and have someone get medical help if possible. Victim should be moved to a sheltered area, warm or at least out of the wind, while still continuing CPR. Once in shelter, remove victim's wet clothing and wrap victim in dry blankets. To get a truly accurate temperature reading, a rectal hypothermic thermometer is required, placed approximately one inch into the rectum. A core body temperature below 90.5 degrees F is very dangerous and difficult to rewarm. If the victim is alert, warm them by skin to skin contact, wrapping both individuals in blankets, administering sips of warm liquid. Encourage the victim to gently exercise by moving any body part that will not cause the victim to strain. Seek medical attention immediately.

• Seasickness

The best way to avoid being seasick is to take preventive measures. If you are prone to seasickness you may need to follow a number of the following suggestions:

1) Avoid alcoholic beverages, but keep your body well hydrated with fluids such as fruit juices, soda and sports drinks.
2) Over the counter medications such as Dramamine or the application of a scopolamine patch before departure will prove to be quite helpful.
3) Avoid cramped areas or close quarters.

Procedures:
Once you have the symptoms of seasickness, exposure to fresh air and fixing your view on a stationary point such as an island or an area of land will usually calm the stomach. Treatment of seasickness is necessary in one form or another; if left untreated it could progress to severe dehydration causing the person to become faint or confused, followed by a rapid heartbeat which could lead to other problems.

• Bites and Stings

One of the most common stings is that of the **jellyfish**. After the sting, the tentacles will be left imbedded in the skin causing long lasting pain and infection. The application of a caking formula such as baking soda and water or shaving cream can be applied to lift the tentacles and can later be gently brushed off. Also soak the area in a solution of diluted vinegar to discharge any remaining venom. A final application of an anti-itching cream will relieve itching and burning symptoms. All of these procedures do not need to be performed, but you may see better results if they are followed in this order.

Sea urchins, starfish, sea cucumbers, coral and **barnacles** all produce a dirty wound which can cause infection fairly easily. Removal of the spine or whatever is embedded will often relieve the majority of the pain. Follow this with a sterile cleaning and an antibiotic ointment, and a sterile dressing if needed.

Stings from various fish will produce a painful and possibly life-threatening situation. **Sea snakes** and **stingrays** are some of the common culprits. Their stings or bites can cause severe bruising, redness, and pain, and can be accompanied by weakness and paralysis. In many cases, antivenom is needed, but the onset of symptoms can be slowed to a minimum. Sea snake bites will require a compressive dressing to be applied while immobilizing the affected area. Seek medical attention immediately. Stingray barbs are often imbedded too deep to remove and it is best left to trained medical personnel to remove them. Meanwhile, soaking the area in warm water will alleviate much of the pain and dilute the venom. In most cases, the pain proves to be the worst effect, but you should always discuss the incident with a trained professional.

• Bleeding

Bleeding is usually easy to see, but sometimes the bleeding is internal and will only be evident by signs of shock. First, examine the person for evidence of bleeding and then take the following steps to prevent additional loss of blood:

1) Identify the location of bleeding area.

2) Apply continuous, direct pressure over the bleeding area with a pad or even your hand if necessary. NOTE: If seepage occurs, increase the padding and the pressure.

3) If there are no broken bones and no major pain, raise the wounded area above the level of the heart, still applying pressure. This will help to reduce bleeding.

4) Support the elevated area.

5) Use binding of some kind to hold the padded pressure, if there is bleeding in other areas.

6) If you have learned the location of the major blood vessel which controls blood flow to the area, and direct pressure seems ineffective, apply pressure over the appropriate vessel to stem hemorrhage.

7) Keep the person warm and comfortably quiet until help arrives. *NOTE: People who are bleeding are often frightened and anxiety contributes to the development of shock. Continued reassurance is essential.*

• Near Drowning

When the victim is lacking respiration due to a near drowning:

1) Place the victim's head slightly lower than the body; this will help drainage of the lungs, reducing the risk of re-inhaling the fluids. The draining water will exit through the mouth and nose. Be sure to keep the victim's head turned to one side, which will keep the liquid from returning to the lungs. *NOTE: If there is a suspected neck injury, remember to roll the head and body together, keeping them in alignment.*

2) The victim may begin to breath on his own, beginning by coughing or gasping for air; this is a good sign.

3) If victim is not breathing, begin rescue breathing or if there's no pulse or respiration, begin CPR. *NOTE: Seek medical attention immediately. If none is available, watch victim carefully for 24 hours and seek medical attention at first chance.*

Rules and Regulations

Florida Residents

When applied to a saltwater fishing license, you are a Florida resident if you:

- Have lived continuously in Florida for six months.
- Have established legal residence in Florida.
- Are a member of the United States Armed Forces stationed in Florida.
- Are a student enrolled at a college or university in Florida.

FLORIDA RESIDENT LICENSES*
Ten-Day License $10.00
One-Year License $12.00
Five-Year License $60.00

*Service charge not included

Tax Collectors and the bait and tackle shops who are their agents will assess an additional service charge of $1.50 or $2.00 respectively.

Florida residents may buy a Lifetime Saltwater Fishing License, or a Lifetime Sportsman License. Holders of Lifetime Saltwater Fishing Licenses may fish in saltwater, for their lifetime at no additional fee. The fee includes the taking of snook or crawfish, which would otherwise require a separate fee. A Lifetime Sportsman License allows holders to fish in freshwater of saltwater and to hunt in Florida. Both require holders to obey fishing or hunting laws in effect at any given time. Costs are:

LIFETIME SALTWATER FISHING*
Age 0-4 .... $125.00
Age 5-12 .... $225.00
Age 13-64 .... $300.00
Age 65 or older .... None

LIFETIME SPORTSMAN*
Age 0-4 .... $400.00
Age 5-12 .... $700.00
Age 13-63 .... $1,000.00
Age 64 or older $12.00

Saltwater fishing licenses are sold at all county tax collector's offices, and at many bait-and-tackle shops.

NON-RESIDENT LICENSES*

Three-Day License $5.00
Seven-Day License $15.00
One-Year License $30.00

You Do Not Need a License if You Are:

- A Florida resident fishing from land or a structure fixed to the land – a pier, bridge, dock, floating dock, or jetty or similar structure, but not a boat.

- A Florida resident who is 65 years or older.

- A Florida resident who is a member of the United States Armed Forces stationed outside of Florida and home on leave for 30 days or less. (You must submit your orders as proof.)

- A Florida resident fishing for saltwater fish in freshwater from land or from a structure fixed to the land.

- Under 16 years of age.

- Fishing from a boat which has a valid recreational vessel saltwater fishing license.

- A non-resident fishing from a pier which has a valid pier saltwater-fishing license.

- Holder of a valid commercial saltwater products license – other than the owner, operator, or custodian of a vessel for which a saltwater fishing license is required. (Only one person fishing under a vessel saltwater products license may claim the exemption at any time.)

- Accepted by the Florida Dpeartment of Health and Rehabilitative Services (HRS) for developmental services, or assigned by a court to an HRS rehabilitation program that involves training in Florida aquatic resources.

- A Florida resident who is permanently and totally disabled may obtain a permanent saltwater fishing license at no charge from a county tax collector.

OTHER SALTWATER FISHING FEES

Vessel licenses are required for all vessels which charge a fee to take passengers out to catch marine fish.

Eleven or more customers .. $800.00
Five to ten customers $400.00
Four or less customers $200.00

Optional fees include the annual Recreational Vessel fee ($2,000) for not-for-hire pleasure craft and the annual Pier license, ($500.00) for piers that charge an access fee.

Additional Privilege Stamp
Snook Stamp $2.00
Crawfish Stamp $2.00

If you are exempt from licenses, you are exempt from stamps.

The money collected from saltwater fishing licenses is used to improve and restore fish habitat, and for marine fisheries research, law enforcement and public education on marine resources.

Basic Recreational Saltwater Fishing Regulations

Species	Size Limit	Closed Season
Amberjack-Greater 1 R	28" fork	***
Billfish	Sailfish 57" Blue Marlin 86" White Marlin 62"	***
Black Drum 1 R	Not less than 14" or more than 24"	***
Black Mullet R	***	10 consecutive 24 hr. period beginning at noon on 4th Frid in December
Bluefish 1 R	12" fork	***
Bonefish	18"	***
Clams – Hard	1" thick at hinge	***
Cobia (Ling) 1	33" fork	***
Crab – Blue R S	***	***
Crab – Stone R S	2 3/4" claw	May 15 to October 15
Crawfish R S	More than 3" carapace	April 1 to August 5 Exception: sportsman season last successive Wed. & Thurs of July each year
Dolphin 2	***	***
Flounder R 1 2	12"	***
Grey Trigger 1 2	12"	***
Grouper R 1 2	20"	***
Grouper – Warsaw R 2	***	***
Hogfish R 2	12" fork	***
Mackerel – King R	20" fork	***
Mackerel – Spanish R 1	12"	***

R – Restricted Species   S – Saltwater Product License
1 – Must remain in whole condition until landed ashore
2 – Gear restrictions apply. Contact nearest FMP.

Daily Rec. Bag Limit	Remarks
3 per person per day	Illegal to sell, purchase or exchange less than 36" fork length. New rule pending.
1 per person per day	Species includes marlin, spearfish and sailfish. Illegal to buy or sell. Federal size limits apply.
5 per person per day	Illegal to possess more than one over 24".
50 per vessel or person, whichever is less	Mullet is not a restricted species west of the Ochlockonee River.
10 per person per day	
1 per person per day	Illegal to buy or sell. Possession limit one.
– 5 gal. bucket per person or 2 per vessel, whichever is less	Illegal to harvest from closed areas. Call FMP for current information.
2 per person per day	
10 gallons whole	SPL with RS & Blue Crab endorsements required to use over 5 traps. Trap requirements apply. Harvest of egg-bearing Blue Crab prohibited.
al. stone crab claws per person or 2 gal. per vessel, whichever is less	SPL with RS & Blue Crab endorsements required to use over 5 traps. Trap requirements apply. Illegal to possess whole crab.
24 per vessel or 6 per person, whichever is greater	SPL with RS endorsements required to use traps. Crawfish stamp required. Special recreational license holder bag limit – 50. Call FMP for current information on sportsman's season.
10 per person per day	20" size limit for sale.
10 per person per day	May be harvested with a gig.
***	
5 aggregate of all species	Includes Yellowfin, Red, Black, Gag, Yellowmouth, Scamp. Harvest of Nassau and Jewfish prohibited.
1 per vessel	Not counted in Grouper aggregate bag limit.
5 per person per day	
2 per person per day	Bag limit in Gulf-Atlantic fishery reduced to 1 when federal waters are closed to all harvest.
10 per person per day	Length is measured from tip of nose to rear center of tail. Transfer of Spanish Mackerel to other vessels is prohibited.

Since local regulations governing the taking of saltwater products may exist, you should contact the Florida Marine Patrol (FMP) Field Office nearest the location where you will be engaging in these activities.

Basic Recreational Saltwater Fishing Regulations, cont.

Species	Size Limit	Closed Season
Oysters	3"	June, July, August in Dixie, Wakulla, counties. July, August, Sept. in all other
Permit R 1 2	Not less than 10" or more than 20"	***
Pompano R 1 2	Not less than 10" or more than 20"	***
Pompano-African R 1	Not less than 24"	***
Red Drum (Redfish) 1 2	Not less than 18" or more than 27"	***
Red Porgy 1 2	12" on Atlantic coast	***
Scallops – Bay	***	September 1 to June 30
Sea Bass 1 2	8"	***
Shad	***	March 15 to November 1
Shark	***	***
Sheepshead R 1 2	12"	***
Shrimp	***	***
Snapper – Cubera R 1 2	Not less than 12" or more than 30"	***
Snapper – Gray (Mangrove) R 1 2	10"	***
Snapper – Lane R 1 2	8"	***
Snapper – Mutton R 1 2	16"	***
Snapper – Red R 1 2	15" Gulf / 20" Atlantic	***
Snapper – Schoolmaster R 1 2	10"	***
Snapper – Vermilion R 1 2	8" Gulf / 10" Atlantic	***
Snapper – All Other R 1 2	12"	***
Snook 1 2	Not less than 24" or more than 34"	Dec. 15 to Jan. 31 of each y & June, July & August
Speckled Hind R	***	***
Spotted Sea Trout R 1 2	E/SW Regions: not less than 15" – not more than 20" NW Region: not less than 15" – not more than 24"	E/SW Regions: Closed Nov. & NW Region: Closed Feb.

R – Restricted Species   S – Saltwater Product License

Daily Rec. Bag Limit	Remarks
2 bags per person or vessel, whichever is less per day	Apalachicola Bay has summer & winter seasons. Harvest from approved shellfish areas only. Call FMP for current info.
10 per person per day	May possess one over 20". Aggregate bag limit of 10 Pompano or Permit per person per day.
10 fish per day per vessel	May possess one over 20". Aggregate bag limit of 10 Pompano or Permit per person per day.
2 per vessel or person, whichever is less	Hook and line gear only.
1 per person per day	Gigging, spearing, snatching prohibited. Illegal to buy or sell native Red Drum.
***	***
2 gallons whole or 1 pint meat	Restricted harvest areas apply to certain state waters. Call FMP for current information.
***	
10 per person per day	Hook and line gear only.
1 per person/2 per vessel whichever is less	Protected species. Practice of finning prohibited.
10 per person per day	Sheepshead may not be harvested by a gig.
5 gallons heads on	Must be landed in a whole condition.
10 per person per day	No more than 2 – 30" or larger per person or vessel whichever is less. Under 30" not included in aggregate bag limit.
5 per person per day	No more than 10 snappers aggregate of all snappers with a bag limit.
ag limit applies toward aggregate of all snappers if harvested in **Atlantic**.	Lane Snapper harvested in **Gulf of Mexico** not subject to aggregate bag limit.
10 per person per day	No more than 10 snappers aggregate of all snappers with a bag limit.
2 Atlantic / 5 Gulf of Mexico	No more than 10 snappers aggregate of all snappers with a bag limit.
10 per person per day	No more than 10 snappers aggregate of all snappers with a bag limit.
*** (Gulf) / 10 (Atlantic)	Not counted in Snapper aggregate bag limit.
10 aggregate of all snapper having a bag limit	Includes Blackfin, Cubera under 30", Dog, Mahogany, Queen, Silk and Yellowtail.
2 per person per day	Illegal to possess more than one over 34". Illegal to buy or sell. Snook stamp required.
1 per person per vessel	Not counted in Grouper aggregate bag limit.
W Regions: 5 fish per person per day W Region: 7 fish per person per day	May possess one fish over the maximum size limit. Call FMP for information regarding regional boundaries.

1 – Must remain in whole condition until landed ashore
2 – Gear restrictions apply. Contact nearest FMP.

Basic Recreational Saltwater Fishing Regulations, cont

Species	Size Limit	Closed Season
Tarpon	***	***
Tripletail R 1	15"	***
Weakfish R 1	12"	***

R – Restricted Species   S – Saltwater Product License

ORNAMENTAL TROPICAL FISH/PLANTS

MINIMUM SIZE LIMIT
(total length)

Spanish Hogfish 2"

MAXIMUM SIZE LIMIT
(total length)

Angelfish (except rock beauty) 8"
Butterfly, Jawfish 4"
Rock Beauty 5"
Gobies 2"
Spanish Hogfish 8"
Spotfin Hogfish 8"

BAG LIMIT
(total length)

Fishes / Invertebrates: 20 per person per day.
No more than 5 Angelfish and no more than 6
Octocoral colonies.
Plants: 1 gallon per person per day.

*Live landing and live well requirements. Harvest in
Biscayne National Park prohibited. Unlawful to
harvest or possess Longspine Urchin and Bahama
Starfish. Harvest of live rock in state waters is
prohibited.*

PROTECTED SPECIES
*It is unlawful to harvest, possess, land, purchase, sell
or exchange the following species:*
Jewfish, Sawfish, Sawshark, Basking Shark, Whale Shark, Spotted Eagle Ray,
Sturgeon, Nassau Grouper

Daily Rec. Bag Limit	Remarks
2 per person per day	Illegal to buy or sell – requires $50 tarpon tag to possess or kill.
2 per person per day	Hook and line gear only.
4 per person per day	

1 – Must remain in whole condition until landed ashore
2 – Gear restrictions apply. Contact nearest FMP.

TELEPHONE NUMBERS FOR MARINE PATROL FIELD OFFICES

Dist. 1
Jacksonville Beach (904) 270-2500
Titusville (407) 383-2740

Dist. 2
Miami (305) 325-3346
Jupiter (407) 624-6935

Dist. 3
Marathon (305) 289-2323
Ft. Myers (941) 332-6971

Dist. 4
Tampa (813) 272-2516
Crystal River (352) 447-1633

Dist. 5
Panama City (904) 233-5150
Pensacola (904) 444-8978
Carrabelle (904) 697-3741

In emergencies, or if state saltwater fishing laws are being violated – call **1-800-DIALFMP**, or for cellular phone users throughout the state, ***FMP**

A Guide to Florida's Waterway Signs and Markers

Slow Speed Minimum Wake and **Slow Down Minimum Wake** *mean the same thing.*

Slow Speed/Minimum Wake

requires that all vessels be completely off plane and fully settled into the water. The vessels may then proceed at a speed which is reasonable and prudent under the existing circumstances.

The purpose of this restriction is to regulate vessel speed, not the size of a vessel's wake.

How do I know if I am travelling at Slow Speed Minimum Wake?

If your vessel is operating on a plane (i.e. travels on the top of the water), you are not operating at slow speed minimum wake.

If your vessel is in process of coming off of plane and settling into the water you are not operating at slow speed minimum wake.

If your vessel is travelling at such a speed that there is little or no wake and *is completely settled* into the water, you are travelling at Slow Speed Minimum Wake.

Idle Speed/No Wake

is the most restrictive of vessel speed. This restriction prohibits the operation of vessels at any speed greater than that speed which is necessary to maintain steerage. An example of idle speed/no wake would be a car with an automatic transmission that is placed in "drive" but

is given neither gas nor brake; the engine will "idle" and the car will creep forward at very low speed.

Idle Speed/No Wake will vary from one vessel to another depending on the particular vessel's size, shape, power system, and steering configuration. It will also vary for any given vessel depending on that vessel's load, the wind direction and speed, and the sea conditions. Generally, however, it will be between 1 and 3 miles per hour for outboard and inboard/outdrive type vessels, and between 2 and 5 miles per hour for fixed shaft/rudder vessels.

Idle Speed/No Wake is usually reserved for areas with a high risk of collision and specific locations with high probability of damage and injury from vessel wake.

These areas include but are not limited to blind intersections, bridge fender systems, boat ramps, and fueling facilities.

The speed at which you dock your vessel is Idle Speed No Wake.

Vessel Wake is the movement of waves created by the motion of the vessel. It is the track or path that the vessel leaves behind it.

*For vessel wake information in **Broward County only,** see below:*

The maximum allowable wake created by any vessel, regardless of speed or size of vessel is 15" in vertical height, measured at least 25' from the vessel.

Regulatory Markers

A vertical diamond shape of international orange with white center indicate **DANGER**. The type of danger will be indicated by words or well-known abbreviations in block letters inside the diamond shape.

A vertical diamond shape of international orange with a cross of the same color within it against a white center without qualifying information shall indicate a zone from which all vessels are excluded. An explanation may be placed outside of the crossed area.

A circle of international orange with a white center will indicate a control or restriction. The type of the control or restriction will be indicated by words, numerals. Well known abbreviations may be inside the circle.

A rectangle or square shape of international orange with a white center will indicate information such as directions, distances and locations. The message shall be presented within a rectangle in black letters.

• Lateral Buoys

The Lateral System employs a simple arrangement of shapes and colors to indicate the side on which a buoy should be passed when proceeding in a given direction.

In Florida and the United States when proceeding in a southerly direction along the Atlantic Coast, or in a northerly and westerly direction along the Gulf of Mexico, the red buoy will be on your right, green on left. This can be remembered as proceeding around the coastline of Florida in a clockwise direction.

Buoy Shapes – (from seaward) Port buoys will be a rectangular green marker or a can-type buoy. Starboard buoys will be a triangular red marker or can-type buoy.

• Definitions

Green Buoy – marks the left (or port) side of a channel when entering from seaward, and must be passed by keeping the buoy on the left side.

Red Buoy – marks the right (or starboard) side of a channel, when entering from seaward, and must be passed by keeping the buoy on the right side.

Port Side – Left side of vessel when coming from seaward. Colors, Numbers, Lights and Reflectors shall be as follows: Color:Green; Number(s); Odd; Lights: Flashing Green; Reflector(s): Green.

Starboard Side – Right side of vessel when coming from seaward (red, right, returning). Colors, Numbers, Lights, and Reflectors shall be as follows: Color: Red; Number(s): Even; Lights: Flashing Red; Reflector(s): Red.

• Maneuvering

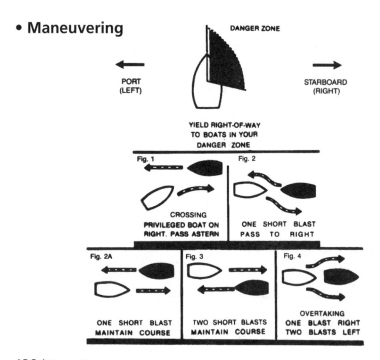

Minimum Required Safety Equipment for Recreational Boats

Equipment	Class A less than 16 ft. less than 4.9 m	Class 1 16 to less than 26 ft. 4.9 to less than 7.9 m	Class 2 26 to less than 40 ft. 7.9 to less than 12.2 m	Class 3 40 to less than 65 ft. 12.2 to not more than 19.8 m
PERSONAL FLOTATION DEVICES (PFDS) Must say USCG Approved, Must be in serviceable condition Must be properly stowed.	One approved Type I, II, or III PFD for each person on board or being towed on water skis, etc.			
	NOTE: A type V hybrid PFD may be substituted for a Type I, II, III device but it must be actually worn whenever the vessel is under way and the person is not in the cabin or other enclosed area. Class A and Class 1: Every person under six years of age on board must wear an approved Type I, II, or III PFD while vessel is under way. PERSONAL WATERCRAFT: Every person operating, riding on, or being towed behind must wear an approved Type I, II, III, or V PFD. SKIER: Every person skiing or aquaplaning must wear an approved Type I, II, or III PFD.		One approved Type I, II, or III PFD for each person on board or being towed on water skis, etc.; and in addition, one throwable Type IV device.	
FIRE EXTINGUISHER Must say USCG Approved, Must be in serviceable condition.	At least one B-I type approved hand portable fire extinguisher. (Not required on outboard motorboats less than 26 feet in length and not carrying passengers for hire if the construction of such motorboats will not permit entrapment of explosive or flammable gasses or vapors and if fuel tanks are not permanently installed.		At least two B-I type approved hand portable fire extinguishers OR at least one B-II type approved hand portable fire extinguisher.	At least three B-I type approved hand portable fire extinguishers OR at least one B-II type approved hand portable fire extinguishers.
	NOTE: When an approved fixed fire extinguisher system is installed in machinery space(s), it may be counted in place of one B-I type hand portable fire extinguisher. Some fire extinguishers require specific mounting brackets for approval. Read the label on your fire extinguisher for this information.			
VISUAL DISTRESS SIGNAL Required on the high sea and coastal waters only.	Must carry approved visual distress signals for nighttime use.	Must carry visual distress signals approved for both daytime and nighttime use.		
	NOTE: Coastal waters means the Atlantic Ocean, Gulf of Mexico, and all bays, sounds, harbors, rivers, inlets, etc., where any entrance is over 2 miles wide to the first point where the distance between shorelines narrows to 2 miles.			
BELL AND WHISTLE (SOUND PRODUCING DEVICES)	Every vessel less than 12 meters (39.4 ft.) in length must carry an efficient sound producing device. The sound producing device need not meet any particular specification, as long as the vessel can produce the signals required by the Navigation Rules. The public may purchase a copy of the Navigation Rules from the U.S. Government Printing Office (GPO) at GPO bookstores located in many cities, from GPO sales agents located in principal ports or by telephone at (202) 783-3238. The book is also available for order by mail from : Superintendent of Documents, U.S. Government Printing Office, Washington, D.C. 20402.			Every vessel 12 meters (39.4 ft.) but less than 20 meters (65.6 ft.) in length must carry a whistle and bell. The whistle must be audible for 1/2 nautical mile. The mouth of the bell must be at least 200 mm (7.87 inches) in diameter.
BACKFIRE FLAME CONTROL	An effective means of controlling backfire flame of all gasoline engines installed after April 25, 1940, except outboard motors. Backfire flame arresters must be USCG approved.			
VENTILATION Boats built before August 1, 1980.	At least two ventilator ducts fitted with cowls or their equivalent for the purpose of properly and efficiently ventilating the bilges of every closed engine and fuel tank compartment of boats constructed or decked over after April 25, 1940, using gasoline as fuel or other fuels having a flash point of 110° or less.			
VENTILATION Boats built on August 1, 1980 or later.	At least two ventilator ducts for the purpose of efficiently ventilating every closed compartment that contains a gasoline engine and every closed compartment containing a gasoline tank, except those having permanently installed tanks which vent outside the boat and contain no unprotected electrical devices. Also, engine compartments containing a gasoline engine having a cranking motor must contain power operated exhaust blowers which can be controlled from the instrument panel.			

VHF Radio Operation Guidelines

The following rules and regulations are not a complete list. We have listed some of them to serve as a helpful guide; all users of a VHF radio of any type must have their equipment licensed.

Be sure to use the proper channel when transmitting; you must use only authorized channels! The following guide will explain the operations for each channel.

Channel 16 is reserved for distress and safety communications. You may make brief contact with another vessel or marine coast station, however, after contact you must switch to a 'working frequency' to complete your message.

Voice communication is prohibited on Channel 70. This channel is reserved and mandated by international maritime treaty. It is an automated digital selective calling channel.

Frequent radio checks tie up the airways so be sure to use a working frequency. Do not call the Coast Guard or use Channel 16 for radio checks.

FCC regulates equipment that may be used, required licenses, contents of messages aired, and many other radio operations. Be sure you are operating legally and know the guidelines for transmitting a message. Misuse of marine radio can carry a stiff penalty.

CHANNEL	VESSEL TRANSMIT	VESSEL RECEIVE	OPERATIONS
01	156.050	156.050	Port & Commercial
03	156.150	156.150	Port & Commercial
05	156.250	156.250	Port Operations
06	156.300	156.300	Intership Safety
07	156.350	156.350	Commercial
08	156.400	156.400	Commercial
09	156.450	156.450	Commercial/Noncom.
10	156.500	156.500	Commercial
11	156.550	156.550	Commercial
12	156.600	156.600	Port Operations
13	156.650	156.650	Nav. (Bridge-Bridge)
14	156.700	156.700	Port Operations
15	156.750	156.750	Environmental (Receive)
16	156.800	156.800	Distress/Safety Calling
17	156.850	156.850	State Control
18	156.900	156.900	Commercial
19	156.950	156.950	Commercial
20	157.000	161.600	Port Operations
21	157.050	157.050	US Government Only
22	157.100	157.100	US Coast Guard Only
23	157.150	157.150	US Government Only
24	157.200	161.800	Public Correspondence
25	157.250	161.850	Public Correspondence
26	157.300	161.900	Public Correspondence
27	157.350	161.950	Public Correspondence
28	157.400	162.000	Public Correspondence
65	156.275	156.275	Port Operations
66	156.325	156.325	Port Operations
67	156.375	156.375	Commercial
68	156.425	156.425	Non-Commercial
69	156.475	156.475	Non-Commercial
70	156.525	156.525	Data-Computer Only
71	156.575	156.575	Non-Commercial
72	156.625	156.625	Non-Commercial
73	156.675	156.675	Port Operations

CHANNEL	VESSEL TRANSMIT	VESSEL RECEIVE	OPERATIONS
74	156.725	156.725	Port Operations
77	156.875	156.875	Port Operations
78	156.925	156.925	Non-Commercial
79	156.975	156.975	Commercial
80	157.025	157.025	Commercial
81	157.075	157.075	US Government Only
82	157.125	157.125	US Government Only
83	157.175	157.175	US Government Only
84	157.225	161.825	Public Correspondence
85			Public Correspondence
86	157.325	161.925	Public Correspondence
87	157.375	161.975	Public Correspondence
88	157.425	162.025	Public Correspondence
89			Commercial
WX1	No Transmit	162.550	Weather (Receive Only)
WX2	No Transmit	162.400	Weather (Receive Only)
WX3	No Transmit	162.475	Weather (Receive Only)

Artificial Reef Atlas

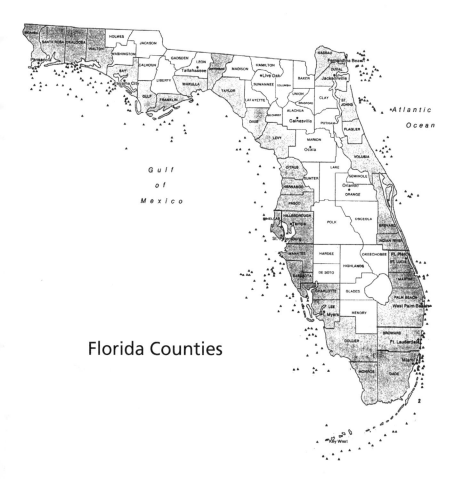

Florida Counties

Artificial reefs use recycled materials to create underwater habitats for marine life. These reefs allow a host of fish, algae and other sea creatures to flourish in areas where they otherwise wouldn't. Florida's Artificial Reef Program requires the efforts of specially-trained employees to successfully construct and monitor the reefs year-round.

Reef Coordinates

Bay County

Reef Name	Depth	Loran 1	Loran 2	Description
• Highway 79 Bridge	74	14031.0	46973.4	400 cubic yards of concrete bridge spans
• The Black Bart	79	14030.0	46972.6	180' oil supply ship
• Highway 79 Bridge	74	14029.7	46972.3	400 cubic yards of concrete bridge spans
• Reef Ex East Site	95	13999.6	46940.1	3 M60 Army tanks located around center coordinates
• Reef Ex Center Site	95	13994.4	46945.5	5 M60 Army tanks located around center coordinates
• B.J. Putnam Reef	103	13991.6	46909.1	174' steel ship "B.J. Putnam"
• Reef Ex West Site	95	13990.4	46950,4	5 M60 Army tanks located around center coordinates

Brevard County

Reef Name	Depth	Loran 1	Loran 2	Description
• Brevard Reef Site	60	43866.0	61920.0	148' vessel "Damocles" sunk w/misc. concrete, dumpsters & scrap metal
• Hummingbird Reef	110	43866.2	61898.8	Concrete & steel rubble, Launch pad material
• Brevard Artificial Reef	60	43865.1	61926.7	140 concrete reef balls
• Tiger Red	85	43842.0	61926.0	Cut up tug boat "Tiger Red"
• Canaveral Site #1	70	43812.5	61887.5	30' diameter storage tank, 4 other tanks

Reef Name	Depth	Loran 1	Loran 2	Description
• Canaveral Site #1	70	43789.9	61900.2	Four steel tanks secured to barge with cable
• FP&L/FIT Experiment. Reef	38	43462.0	62038.0	Oil ash/concrete blocks

Broward County

Reef Name	Depth	Loran 1	Loran 2	Description
• Ancient Mariner	70	14281.0	62088.6	USCG Cutter "Nemesis"
• Berry Patch	65	14281.1	62088.5	65' tug, 2 other vessels
• Papa's Reef	265	14274.8	62092.6	170' steel ship, "Ebbtide"
• Miller Light (Rodeo)	155	14274.5	62094.1	186' German freighter
• Ronald B. Johnson (Rodeo)	230	14274.3	62093.3	226' Dutch bulk carrie
• Vietnam Veterans' Reef	240	14274.3	62093.3	230' ship named for Ronald B. Johnson and other soldiers who died in the Vietnam War
• Mariner Outboard II	125	14274.3	62094.9	120' ship and 130' ship in very close proximity, both upright
• Rodeo 25	122	14273.8	62095.3	215' steel ship, "Windward Trader"
• Jim Torgerson Reef	120	14273.4	62095.9	160' U.S. Naval support vessel
• Renegade (Rodeo)	190	14273.4	62094.6	150' Dutch freighter
• Lowrance (Rodeo)	200	14272.8	62096.4	435' Canadian freighter
• Captain Dan (Rodeo)	110	14272.3	62096.9	175' Coast Guard buoy tender
• Mako Reef (Rodeo)	240	14272.0	62096.2	Numerous boat molds
• Mercedes	97	14265.2	62105.2	198' German freighter "Mercedes"
• Wendy Rossheim Memorial	65	14264.7	62106.7	118' steel yacht, "Our House III"

Broward County, cont.

Reef Name	Depth	Loran 1	Loran 2	Description
• Grouper Grotto	150	14263.6	62104.5	Fuel tanks, concrete culvert, dredge pipes
• Hog Heaven	60	14262.7	62108.8	Derelict barge: 170' x 70' x 11'

Charlotte County

Reef Name	Depth	Loran 1	Loran 2	Description
• Charlotte Harbour #1	12	14162.8	44024.7	800 tons concrete culverts & concrete sewer boxes
• Cape Haze Reef	25	14144.7	44039.7	21 custom-fabricated modules made of concrete and steel
• M14	43	14126.3	44209.7	746 tons concrete culverts and concrete boxes

Citrus County

Reef Name	Depth	Loran 1	Loran 2	Description
• Fish Haven	30	14356.8	45305.8	500 cubic yards of concrete rubble
• Fish Haven	30	14356.8	45305.5	2000 cubic yards of concrete rubble
• Fish Haven	30	14356.2	45305.5	400 cubic yards of concrete rubble
• Fish Haven	30	14356.2	45305.5	400 tons concrete rubble
• Fish Haven	30	14356.0	45305.0	750 cubic yards of concrete rubble
• Fish Haven	30	14356.0	45305.0	16 hollow concrete junction boxes
• Fish Haven	30	14355.0	45304.4	36 fiberglass boat molds
• Fish Haven	30	14355.0	45304.4	1300 tons of bridge materials and concrete pipes

Collier County

Reef Name	Depth	Loran 1	Loran 2	Description
• Lee/Collier Reef	30	14110.6	43828.0	School buses, Coke and other soft drink trucks
• Naples Pier		14100.4	43768.0	Concrete
• Doctor's Pass Reef	28	14099.1	43800.0	Concrete culverts and two pipe modules
• Doctor's Pass 5 Mile	30	14098.5	43827.6	800 tons concrete culverts
• Gordon's Pass 5 mile reef	25	14090.5	43783.1	DC3 fuselage and concrete culverts
• Pavilion Key Site	18	14090.5	64540.1	Concrete culverts
• Gordon Pass Site	25	14089.8	43777.3	Scattered conc. culverts
• Wiggins Pass 9 Mile	42	14080.5	43912.2	800 tons concrete culverts
• Gordon Pass 9 mile	38	14076.0	43821.9	92 concrete modules set in six rows from N to S
• Caxambas Pass Site	46	14047.3	43774.1	360 tons of concrete culverts

Dade County

Reef Name	Depth	Loran 1	Loran 2	Description
• Site A	240	14246.1	62121.0	257' steel freighter, " Cruz del Sur"
• Liberty Ship	365	14239.4	62123.4	20' Liberty Ship "L. Bodenhamer"
• Haulover Reef	68	14238.9	62129.4	Modules made of concrete pipe surrounded with natural limerock
• Haulover Reef	120	14237.7	62129.4	660 tons concrete culverts
• Andro	103	14237.7	62129.4	165' steel freighter "Andro"
• Patricia	53	14229.5	62136.6	"Patricia" 65' steel tug
• Leon's Barge	50	14229.3	62136.9	"Leon's Barge"100' barge
• John Koppin Mem. Reef	45	14229.3	62137.5	75' steel barge, concrete pipes & girders
• African Queen	44	14229.3	62137.5	"African Queen" 57' steel hull

Dade County, cont.

Reef Name	Depth	Loran 1	Loran 2	Description
• Anchorage Reef	47	14229.3	62137.4	400 tons of large lime-stone boulders, crescent shaped 60' x 125'
• Billy's Barge	48	14228.9	62137.2	"Billy's Barge" 100' barge
• Site E	185	14219.4	62142.2	103' steel freighter, "Mystic Lake"
• Mystic Isle	185	14219.4	62142.2	103' steel ferry "Mystic Isle"
• Star Trek	210	14219.0	62142.2	203' steel ship "Star Trek" FADs
• Proteus	72	14218.7	62144.3	220' steel freighter "Proteus"
• Miracles-Express	55	14218.5	62145.0	"Miracles-Express" 100' steel freighter
• South Seas	73	14218.2	62144.7	175' steel yacht "South Seas"
• Big Lou	55	14217.9	62145.2	"Big Lou" 36' steel hull
• Ultra Freeze	120	14211.1	62150.0	195' steel freighter "Ultra Freeze"
• Hopper Barge	163	14210.3	62149.9	150' steel hopper barge
• Blue Fire	110	14204.6	62155.5	175' steel freighter "Blue Fire"
• Sir Scott	220	14201.2	62157.5	267' steel freighter "Sir Scott", FADs
• Santa Rita	247	14188.9	62170.7	250' steel ship "Santa Rita"
• Belcher Barge	120	14187.0	62174.4	85' steel fuel barge
• Hugo's April Fool	145	14181.7	62180.5	"Danbo" 115' steel freighter
• Site J	140	14181.7	62180.4	287' steel freighter, "Doc de Milly"

Dixie County

Reef Name	Depth	Loran 1	Loran 2	Description
• Horseshoe Reef #1	25	14414.2	45753.1	200 tons of concrete blocks, limestone rock, and railroad arms

Duval County

Reef Name	Depth	Loran 1	Loran 2	Description
• Haddock's Hideaway	67	45252.5	61840.5	190' x 40' barge sunk on site with steel I-beams and rubble on board
• Rabbit's Lair	68	45247.8	61906.9	Steel barge
• Montgomery Reef	68	45232.7	61958.9	63' tug "Reliance"
• Amberjack Hole	80	45210.2	61852.6	Barge
• Busey's Bonanza	65	45195.5	61922.4	Acosta Bridge rubble added to existing reef
• Nine Mile Reef	58	45191.5	61947.6	Vic's 150' barge
• Pablo Grounds	73	45179.2	61969.6	90' barge
• Paul Mains Reef	72	45170.6	61965.8	Navy barge
• Jacksonville Beach Wreck	60	45168.7	62001.7	Culverts
• Middle Ground	75	45130.7	61937.2	Steel tug
• Tournament Reef	110	45128.8	61808.8	230' freighter "Anna"
• Ponte Vedra Grounds	75	45108.0	61982.5	Navy scaffolding
• EEF Site	95	45100.0	61840.5	2000 tons of concrete culverts
• East Ponte Vedra	80	45078.0	61941.0	1250 cubic yards of various concrete items
• Harm's Ledge	90	45077.3	61814.0	150' freighter "Huggins"
• NSS Site	75	45065.5	61865.5	2000 tons of concrete culverts: .5nm WNW of 'Coppedge Reef'
• Blackmar's Reef	106	45040.8	61779.6	Airplane wreck

Escambia County

Reef Name	Depth	Loran 1	Loran 2	Description
• DEP East Site		13268.5	47052.3	5 M60 Army tanks around center coordinates
• County Site #15	82	13256.6	47075.6	48' tug boat
• County Site #15	82	13253.2	47082.6	140' steel barge and steel boxes
•	100	13250.5	47063.3	Concrete & plastic modules, 180' steel ship "Pete Tide II"
• County Site #20	115	13248.4	47007.2	247' dredge boat
• County Site #7		13247.3	47067.1	8 M60 Army tanks around center coordinates

Flagler County

Reef Name	Depth	Loran 1	Loran 2	Description
• Flagler Reef #1	60	44717.4	61978.0	1200 tons of concrete culverts, junction boxes, & manhole sections

Franklin County

Reef Name	Depth	Loran 1	Loran 2	Description
• Carrabelle 3 mile	35	14353.4	46475.7	618 tons of concrete culverts and slab
• Yamaha Reef	85	14313.6	46364.8	195' x 35' x 15' steel barge; 200 tons concrete pilings, one pile at each corner of steel hopper barge

Gulf County

Reef Name	Depth	Loran 1	Loran 2	Description
• Jaycee Reef	45	14115.7	46804.1	Concrete rubble and steel containers
• Virginia Reef	65	14104.0	46815.0	4 boat hulls loaded with metal crates and concrete rubble
• Virginia Reef	65	14104.1	46813.4	Bridge rubble, concrete boxes, and steel hoppers

Hernando County

Reef Name	Depth	Loran 1	Loran 2	Description
• Jim Champion Reef	20	14337.0	45160.0	306 cubic yards of concrete culverts and steel barge
• Jim Champion Reef	20	14336.9	45160.4	650 cubic yards of concrete culverts
• A.H. Richardson	18	14325.6	45109.1	Concrete culverts
• Don Bendickson Reef	25	14319.8	45140.0	10 M60 Army tanks around center coordinates

Hillsborough County

Reef Name	Depth	Loran 1	Loran 2	Description
• Courtney Campbell Reef	16	14267.6	44701.9	Concrete pilings
• Howard Frankland Reef	16	14266.2	44648.5	Pilings, bridge supports
• Picnic Island Reef	26	14253.7	44618.4	830 cubic yards of concrete and misc. fittings
• Bahia Beach Reef	20	14245.8	44561.1	446 tons of concrete forms, rubble and stainless steel mixers
• Bahia Beach Reef	21	14245.7	44560.6	Concrete rubble, concrete slab and clay water pipes

Hillsborough County, cont.

Reef Name	Depth	Loran 1	Loran 2	Description
• Port Manatee Site	17	14225.5	44556.9	632 tons of concrete culverts and pipes
• Ballast Point Pier Reef		5314 Interbay Blvd.		Pier fishermen only
• Egmont Key Reef	17-23	14193.5	44608.0	
• Picnic Island Pier Reef		0.0	0.0	Concrete pyramid modules placed 75' from the end of the picnic pier

Lee County

Reef Name	Depth	Loran 1	Loran 2	Description
• Ft. Myers Wharf		14161.9	43868.1	4800 tons of concrete rubble and rip rap located about 50' offshore
• GH Reef	30	14115.1	43848.9	110' steel barge, 35' steel tugboat, steel dumpsters
• GH Reef	30	14115.1	43848.9	450 tons conc. culverts
• GH Reef	28	14114.7	43851.3	Limestone added to previous materials
• Redfish Pass Reef	24	14108.7	44031.6	Steel barge
• Redfish Pass Reef	22	14109.1	44028.3	Steel barge
• EF (Jaycees) Reef	31	14098.5	43912.0	225 tons conc. culverts
• EF (Jaycees) Reef	31	14097.9	43913.4	300 tons precast concrete
• EF (Jaycees) Reef	31	14097.2	43912.9	310 tons conc. culverts
• 12 Mile Barge Reef	60	14085.3	44111.4	
• Barge #1 Site	57	14083.9	44111.4	ARCOA BIOreef prefabricated units
• Boxcar Reef	72	14082.6	44239.6	CSX boxcars

Reef Name	Depth	Loran 1	Loran 2	Description
• Edison Bridge	40	14078.1	43970.1	14,000 cubic yards of rubble from Edison Bridge
• Deep Reef 1	90	14045.2	44260.0	Two piles of hopper cars, one with 16 cars, the other with 24

Levy County

Reef Name	Depth	Loran 1	Loran 2	Description
• Cedar Key Reef Site 1	23	14398.5	45549.3	Concrete culverts
• Cedar Key Reef Site 2	26	14375.4	45466.4	Four patches of concrete culverts, man hole covers, and boulders
• Cedar Key Reef Site 3	36	14375.0	45640.0	Patches of concrete culverts
• White City Bridge	55	14359.1	45770.2	Steel and concrete rubble from White City Bridge

Manatee County

Reef Name	Depth	Loran 1	Loran 2	Description
• 1 Mile Reef	27	14179.3	44564.2	1000 tons of concrete culverts
• 3 Mile Reef	30	14172.0	44555.0	1100 cubic yards of boat molds, concrete rubble, and solid rubber tires
• 3 Mile Reef	25	14172.0	44555.0	675 tons of concrete culverts
• 3 Mile Reef	30	14172.0	44555.0	300 tons of concrete culverts
• 7 Mile Reef	40	14162.4	44590.5	750 tons of concrete culverts

Martin County

Reef Name	Depth	Loran 1	Loran 2	Description
• Guardian Reef	58	43110.7	62013.4	75' x 25' x 6' barge, large steel tanks, and 1360 tons of concrete culverts
• Bill Donaldson Reef	57	43107.5	62012.5	Various materials including tanks and rinker barrels
• Bill Donaldson Reef	56	43106.5	62012.7	170' steel barge, concrete culverts, cement mixers
• FAD Trolling Alley Reef	250	43100.0	61970.0	FADs, Line out to 43099.9/61965.4
• Al Sirotkin Reef	100	43099.4	61985.4	3000 tons of concrete slabs, pilings, and rubble
• Al Sirotkin Reef	80	43098.9	62008.9	196' steel barge "Mercedes II"
• Dr. Edgar Ernst Reef	60	43063.7	62000.4	2 school bus bodies
• Dr. Edgar Ernst Reef	60	43058.6	62001.6	75,000 concrete weighted tires

Monroe County

Reef Name	Depth	Loran 1	Loran 2	Description
• Marathon Reef Site	100	14033.7	43403.9	Concrete bridge spans
• Big Pine Key Site	18	13984.7	43507.2	Precast concrete shallow reef modules with PVC

Practice a man overboard drill – it might save your life!

Nassau County

Reef Name	Depth	Loran 1	Loran 2	Description
• Whittaker's Snapper Hole	60	45326.8	61915.2	Steel tug
• Whittaker's Snapper Hole	65	45314.4	61907.1	171 tons of concrete culverts, building rubble, misc. steel
• FB6	60	45311.6	61888.3	450 tons of concrete culverts, manholes and junction boxes
• Sahlmans Gulley	60	45308.1	61874.1	Barge
• FC Site	83	45305.0	61895.0	1000 tons of concrete culverts
• FC Site		45293.0	61908.4	Concrete culverts
• FC Site	70	45290.0	61897.0	Concrete culverts
• Fernandina Snapper Banks	70	45292.2	61898.9	Wood boat "Barbett"
• FARF	70	45289.7	61906.4	1000 tons of concrete culverts
• Fernan. Snapper Banks	70	45289.6	61906.5	Concrete culverts

Okaloosa County

Reef Name	Depth	Loran 1	Loran 2	Description
• "C" Leg	60	13772.0	47134.8	S/SE to N/NW chain of concrete pyramids and misc. concrete; loran #s for approx. ctr. of chain
• Fish Haven #3	69	13766.1	47132.6	6 steel storage tanks
• CSX Reef	90	13765.3	47131.8	2 surplus boxcars
• Reef EX Site #8	110	13756.1	47047.8	2 M60 Army tanks around center coordinates
• "A" Leg	60	13718.0	47136.0	East/West chain of concrete pyramids, loran #s for approx. ctr. of chain

Okaloosa County, cont.

Reef Name	Depth	Loran 1	Loran 2	Description
• Reef EX Site #1	70	13663.6	47135.6	2 M60 Army tanks
• CSX Reef	107	13554.8	47067.7	2 surplus boxcars
• Okaloosa County Site #8	109	13532.6	47062.5	7 steel storage tanks around center coordinates

Palm Beach County

Reef Name	Depth	Loran 1	Loran 2	Description
• Miss Jenny		14351.2	62006.4	55' x 50' x 25' dredge barge. 300' south of "Esso Bonaire"
• Classic Barges	200	14335.2	62017.4	Steel barge
• Princess Anne	97	14334.5	62023.2	340' x 58' x 52' steel ferry. Hull has broken into 2 N/S sections
• Tricounty		14330.2	62031.8	188 tons of concrete culverts and catch basins
• Jewfish Ledges		14327.6	62040.0	Deployed May '95 in Lake Worth Lagoon as habitat for snook/jewfish
• Boynton Beach Reef #1	150	14301.2	62066.0	150' freighter "Bud Bar" Culverts
• The Playground	135	14300.5	62065.0	1500 tons of concrete culverts and misc. concrete and steel
• Hydro-Atlantic	166	14284.1	62083.1	325' dredge
• Boca Raton Reef #1	60	14283.3	62085.7	120' freighter "Noula Express"

Pasco County

Reef Name	Depth	Loran 1	Loran 2	Description
• Reef Site #2	40	14276.6	45050.8	10 M60 Army tanks around center coordinates
• Reef Site #1		14275.5	44999.8	110' x 34' x 11' steel barge and 130' x 30' x 7' steel barge
• Reef Site #2	30	14274.7	45048.7	303 tons concrete culverts
• Reef Site #2	30	14274.6	45050.8	800 cubic yards concrete culverts
• Reef Site #1	40	14246.1	44998.9	990 tons of concrete pilings and light posts

Pinellas County

Reef Name	Depth	Loran 1	Loran 2	Description
• Tarpon Springs	26-28	14259.3	44935.6	Live bottom (at S. buoy); artificial reef material
• Dunedin Reef	25-30	14248.1	44887.6	High profile structures; Pyramids 1000' S of buoy
• Pier 60		14245.0	44916.0	Concrete material placed around pilings off Pier 60 in Clearwater
• Clearwater Reef	27-29	14243.5	44859.4	High profile structures
• Rube Allyn Reef		14211.2	44884.6	Concrete culverts and concrete pilings
• Rube Allyn Reef		14211.2	44884.2	Concrete rubble; steel barge; pyramids
• Madeira Beach Reef	30-33	14201.0	44768.0	Low profile; widely scattered material
• Indian Shores Reef	44-46	14200.0	44768.0	2 WWII Navy landing ships; barge
• Treasure Island Reef	29-33	14200.8	44738.7	Large profile pyramid reef

Pinellas County, cont.

Reef Name	Depth	Loran 1	Loran 2	Description
• St. Pete Beach Site	25	14192.9	44704.1	10 M60 Army tanks S/SW of buoy coordinates
• Pinellas (No. 2) Reef	80	14181.6	44943.3	2 180' steel vessels; tug; sight of the *Black Thorn*

Sarasota County

Reef Name	Depth	Loran 1	Loran 2	Description
BAY REEFS:				
• Deamus Hart	10	14181.3	44440.7	Concrete, FPL insulators
• Jim Evans	10	14177.6	44417.9	Concrete, FPL insulators
• Rose Coker	7	14176.9	44404.0	Concrete, FPL insulators
• Pop Jantzen	7	14176.8	44421.1	Concrete, FPL insulators
• O.D. Miller	9-21	14176.5	44430.0	Concrete, FPL insulators
• Bully Powers	12	14173.8	44419.7	Concrete, FPL insulators
OTHER REEFS:				
• Donald Roehr (I3)	22	14169.5	44425.8	Orange Ave Bridge rubble
• Lynn Silvertooth (I1)	30	14166.1	44423.6	Rubble, boxes & piles
• Alan Fisher (I2)	30	14166.1	44437.4	New Pass Bridge rubble, concrete rubble & piles
• M1	42	14155.8	44495.2	Steel barge, fiberglass boats, concrete culvert
• M2	42	14155.1	44490.4	Concrete culverts, boxes & mixer drums
• I4	25	14154.2	44302.6	Venice bridge & pier
• M3	43	14149.8	44480.5	Concrete culverts, boxes & mixer drums
• M4	42	14145.7	44470.7	Concrete rubble

Reef Name	Depth	Loran 1	Loran 2	Description
• M15	38	14143.6	44325.8	Concrete rubble
• M5	43	14141.4	44460.5	Steel barge
• M7-Johnson Reef	50	14137.8	44517.1	Boxcars
• M6	55	14135.4	44451.7	Fiberglass boats, concrete culverts & mixer drums
• M16	49	14134.1	44345.1	Concrete culverts & catch basins
• M8	65	14128.1	44495.5	5 Army tanks, landing craft, boxcars
• M14	43	14126.3	44209.7	Concrete rubble
• M17	63	14124.5	44364.6	'Reef Balls'
• M9	61	14121.0	44400.0	Concrete rubble, 5 tanks
• M10	65	14114.8	44391.5	Sailboat, fiberglass boats, & steel barge
• MD1	80	14109.9 14108.9	44519.1 44518.8	Barge & concrete hopper
• D3	105	14091.9 14091.7	44668.1 44668.4	Boxcars
• D4	103	14090.9	44664.6	Boxcars
• D6	110	14076.8	44579.7	Fiberglass boats & molds
• D9	100	14066.1	44459.5	Steel crane barge & fiberglass boats

(Note: Sarasota County no longer accepts fiberglass boat donations for reef construction)

Bring your used monofilament line back to the dock.

St. John's County

Reef Name	Depth	Loran 1	Loran 2	Description
• Four Mile Reef	60	44986.0	62091.2	Inshore wreck
• Pop Warner Site	66	44961.0	62005.1	2000 tons of concrete culverts
• Nine Mile North Reef	56	44952.2	62026.2	Dumpsters, scattered steel
• Desco Boat	70	44903.1	61975.5	Desco Shrimp Boat
• Desco Wreck Reef	85	44903.0	61976.9	2000 tons of concrete culverts and other precast concrete
• Barge Site	81	44891.7	61958.0	1750 tons of concrete culverts and other precast concrete
• Inner Airplane Site	84	44873.4	61969.8	2000 tons of concrete culverts and 35' LST boat
• McCormick Reef		44858.8	61954.9	65' steel yacht
• Taylor Reef	100	44856.4	62887.8	2500 tons of concrete and fiberglass culverts & other precast concrete
• Shipwreck Reef	70	44818.0	61962.5	2500 tons of concrete culverts and other precast concrete
• South Pinnacle	70	44812.0	61962.5	Freighter
• Offshore St. Augustine Gordon's Wreck		44744.0	61895.2	Gordon's wreck – sailboat

St. Lucie County

Reef Name	Depth	Loran 1	Loran 2	Description
• Ft. Pierce Artificial Reef		44390.0	62039.0	155' steel tug boat, metal tanks, concrete culverts and mixers
• Hutchinson Island	33	44389.5	62040.6	Steel tanks and fiberglass boat hulls

Reef Name	Depth	Loran 1	Loran 2	Description
• Two Bridges Reef	35	43340.0	62038.2	600 tons of concrete bridge material
• Ft. Pierce Fish Haven	37	43334.0	62038.4	200 tons conc. culverts
• Fishing Club Reef	55	43262.0	62005.0	Concrete rubble
• 50' Inshore Reef Site	50	43259.2	62005.2	110' steel barge
• 50' Inshore Reef Site	50	43259.3	62005.1	Ferro hulled cement sailboat
• 50' Inshore Reef Site	50	43259.2	62005.1	190 tons of concrete culverts
• Muliphen-Fishing Club	168	43207.4	61958.4	460' C2 cargo vessel "Muliphen"
• Stan's Reef #1	190	43204.5	61954.2	150' oceangoing tug, FADs
• Stan's Reef #2	150	43200.0	61960.7	65' tug, FADs
• "Beverly M" Reef	58	43199.3	61960.7	65' derelict steel tug boat

Taylor County

Reef Name	Depth	Loran 1	Loran 2	Description
• Birdrack #3	5	14475.1	63249.9	Culverts placed circularly around birdrack
• Birdrack #1	4	14489.7	63283.4	Culverts placed circularly around birdrack
• Birdrack #2	5	14482.5	63271.5	Culverts placed circularly around birdrack
• Steinhatchee Reef	22	14460.2	46009.9	Concrete culverts and mixed metal
• Steinhatchee Reef	22	14460.0	46011.0	Steel scrap and steel boiler parts
• Steinhatchee Reef	22	14459.9	46011.2	Concrete culverts, mixed metal, and boiler parts

Volusia County

Reef Name	Depth	Loran 1	Loran 2	Description
• Rainbow Reef	80	44519.4	61959.1	Concrete houseboat, concrete culverts
• Port Authority Site #4	80	44517.9	61958.5	Concrete and 31' x 7' barge
• Liberty Ship	85	44453.8	61982.3	440' liberty ship "Mindanao"
• Port Authority Site #2	75	44422.1	61963.8	Concrete and car transport trailers
• Cracker Ridge	80	44409.1	61959.0	Barge, concrete culverts, dumpsters
• Port Authority Site #2	75	44406.8	61956.2	1100 concrete culverts
• Port Authority Site #1	25	44397.0	61973.7	970 concrete culverts
• Barge Wreck	73	44156.7	61907.4	350' barge with crane, 150 yds west of buoy

Wakulla County

Reef Name	Depth	Loran 1	Loran 2	Description
• St. Marks Reef	20	14478.0	46426.1	100 cubic yards of concrete culverts, DC-3 plane
• Dog Ballard Reef	26	14476.3	46369.1	253 tons concrete culverts
• Rotary Reef	25	14450.0	46421.0	Concrete culverts and bridge rubble
• OAR/Wakulla DZ #3	56	14397.5	46348.8	Concrete culverts, concrete tanks & misc. conc.
• OAR/Wakulla DZ #3	55	14394.6	46350.0	200 tons of concrete culverts & concrete boxes
• OAR/Wakulla DZ #1	55	14394.6	46350.0	297 tons conc. culverts
• OAR/Wakulla DZ #2	55	14393.6	46353.8	Fiberglass boat molds and bridge materials

Notes on other fishing spots:

Index

A

Appendix A
Grouper

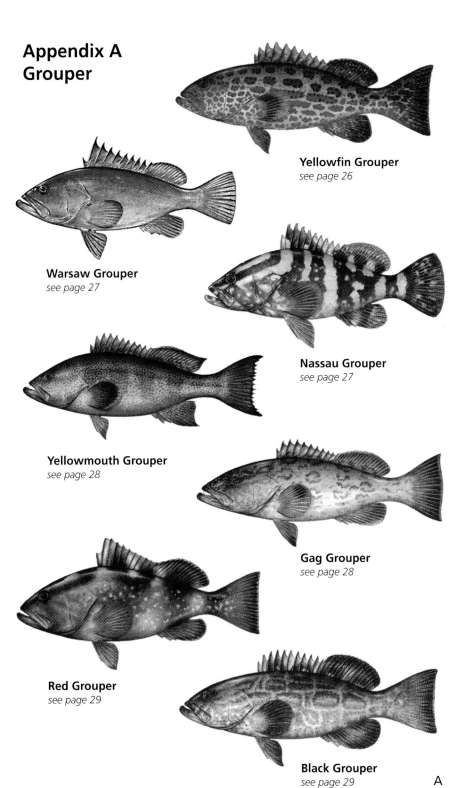

Yellowfin Grouper
see page 26

Warsaw Grouper
see page 27

Nassau Grouper
see page 27

Yellowmouth Grouper
see page 28

Gag Grouper
see page 28

Red Grouper
see page 29

Black Grouper
see page 29

A

Appendix B & C
Snapper

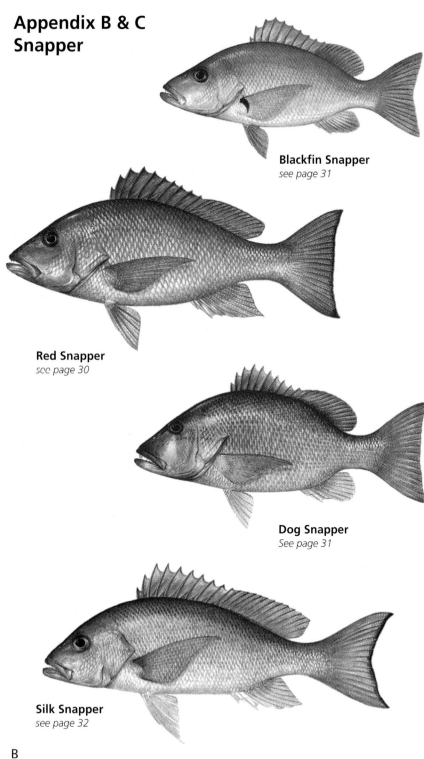

Blackfin Snapper
see page 31

Red Snapper
see page 30

Dog Snapper
See page 31

Silk Snapper
see page 32

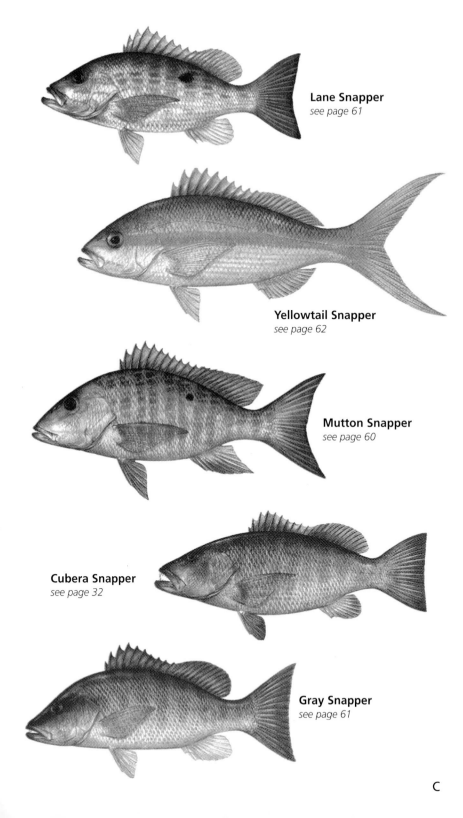

Lane Snapper
see page 61

Yellowtail Snapper
see page 62

Mutton Snapper
see page 60

Cubera Snapper
see page 32

Gray Snapper
see page 61

C

Appendix D

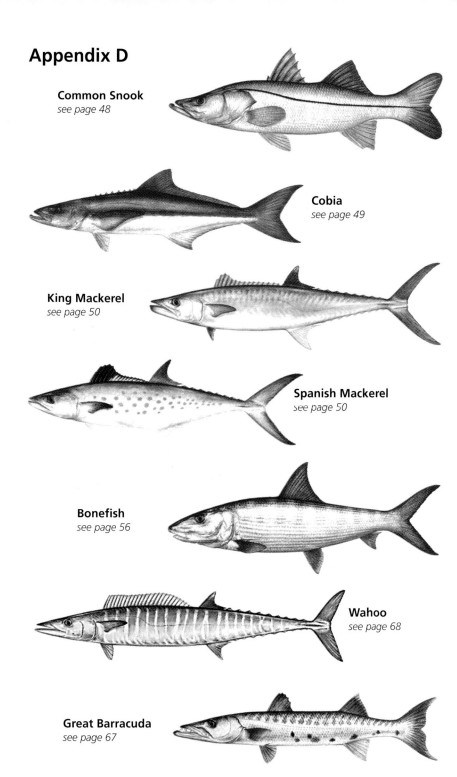

Common Snook
see page 48

Cobia
see page 49

King Mackerel
see page 50

Spanish Mackerel
see page 50

Bonefish
see page 56

Wahoo
see page 68

Great Barracuda
see page 67

D

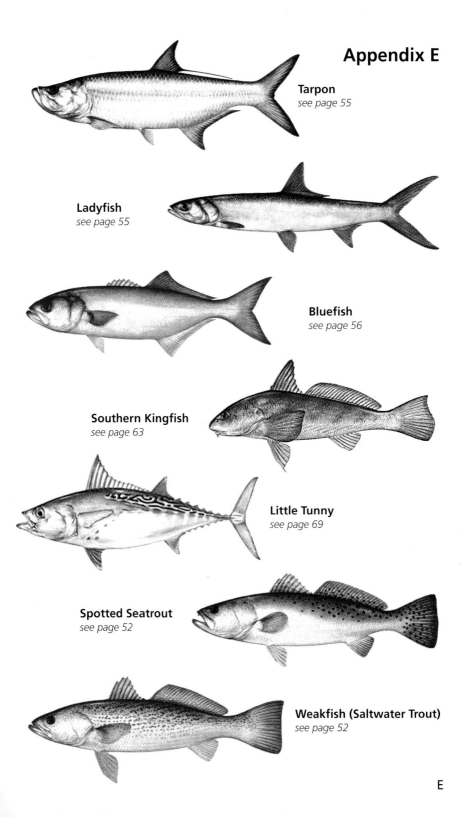

Tarpon
see page 55

Ladyfish
see page 55

Bluefish
see page 56

Southern Kingfish
see page 63

Little Tunny
see page 69

Spotted Seatrout
see page 52

Weakfish (Saltwater Trout)
see page 52

Appendix F

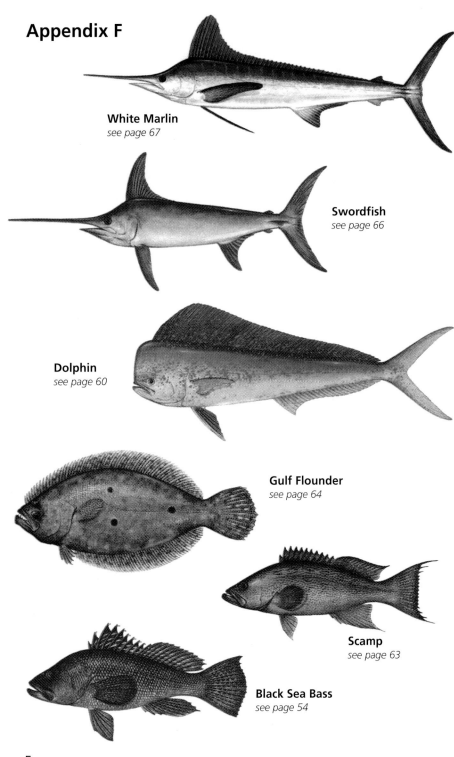

White Marlin
see page 67

Swordfish
see page 66

Dolphin
see page 60

Gulf Flounder
see page 64

Scamp
see page 63

Black Sea Bass
see page 54

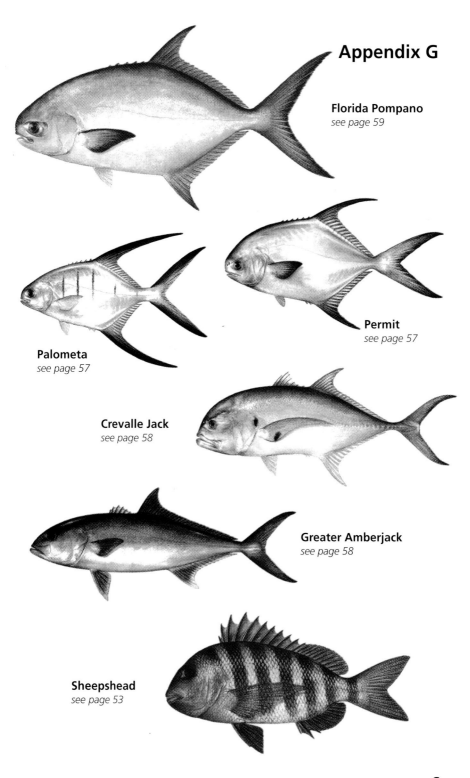

Florida Pompano
see page 59

Permit
see page 57

Palometa
see page 57

Crevalle Jack
see page 58

Greater Amberjack
see page 58

Sheepshead
see page 53

Appendix H

Jewfish
see page 64

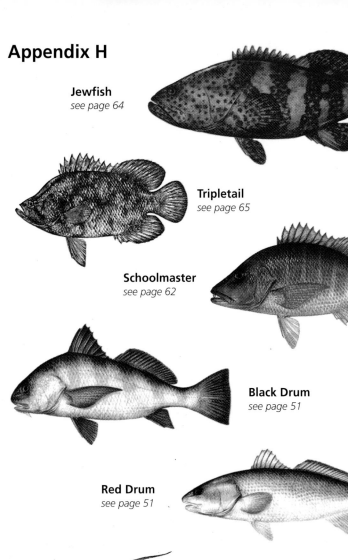

Tripletail
see page 65

Schoolmaster
see page 62

Black Drum
see page 51

Red Drum
see page 51

Gafftopsail Catfish
see page 65

Hardhead Catfish
see page 66

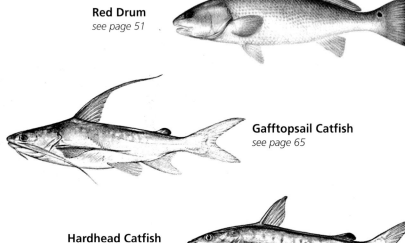

H